Recent Research in Psychology

D1555470

Peter A. Bertocci

The Person and Primary Emotions

•A15042 394062

BF
531
.B47
1988
West

Springer-Verlag
New York Berlin Heidelberg
London Paris Tokyo

Peter A. Bertocci
Borden Parker Bowne Professor Emeritus
    of Philosophy
Boston University
Boston, Massachusetts 02215
USA

Library of Congress Cataloging-in-Publication Data
Bertocci, Peter Anthony.
    The person and primary emotions.
    (Recent research in psychology)
    Bibliography: p.
    Includes index.
    1. Emotions--Philosophy. 2. Motivation (Psychology)
--Philosophy. 3. Philosophical anthropology.
I. Title. II. Series.
BF531.B47   1988   152.4'32   88-19989

© 1988 by Springer-Verlag New York Inc.
All rights reserved. This work may not be translated or copied in whole or in part without the
written permission of the publisher (Springer-Verlag, 175 Fifth Avenue, New York, NY 10010,
USA), except for brief excerpts in connection with reviews or scholarly analysis. Use in
connection with any form of information storage and retrieval, electronic adaptation, computer
software, or by similar or dissimilar methodology now known or hereafter developed is
forbidden.
The use of general descriptive names, trade names, trademarks, etc. in this publication, even if
the former are not especially identified, is not to be taken as a sign that such names, as
understood by the Trade Marks and Merchandise Marks Act, may accordingly be used freely
by anyone.

Camera-ready copy provided by the author.
Printed and bound by Edwards Brothers, Inc., Ann Arbor, Michigan.
Printed in the United States of America.

9 8 7 6 5 4 3 2 1

ISBN 0-387-96812-1 Springer-Verlag New York Berlin Heidelberg
ISBN 3-540-96812-1 Springer-Verlag Berlin Heidelberg New York

To

Gordon Allport
Brand Blanshard
Hywel Lewis
Frederick R. Tennant

No science can be more secure than the unconcious
metaphysics it presupposes.
Alfred North Whitehead
Adventure of Ideas, p. 197.

All books on the psychology of personality are at the same
time books on the philosophy of the person....In most
psychological texts, however, the philosophy is hidden.
Gordon W. Allport
Pattern and Growth in Personality, p. xi.

PREFACE

I shall propose that the unlearned motives of persons are primary emotions. I am not surprised that many informed readers will wonder where I have been for the last five decades when even the conception of unlearned motives (instincts, drives, urges) has been shown to be little more than the result of undisciplined investigation? And here I am proposing that in the nature and dynamics of some emotions that persons experience we can gain more adequate understanding of human motives at the unlearned level.

During the last five decades I have spent most of my time teaching the history of philosophy, metaphysics, philosophy of religion, ethics and theory of value, the psychology of personality, and the philosophy of personality. Increasingly I have paid special attention to the ways in which claims about ˋthe nature of man' influence the theory of motives, emotions, and feelings. What kept impressing me is the way in which the interpretation of the "findings" about motives, feelings, and emotion reflect unargued conceptions of human nature, or that the views of fundamental motives, feelings, and emotions unduly dominate the underlying conception of the person. In focusing attention first on the essential nature of a person I shall be discussing issues that are actually basic to our more analytical interpretation of the nature and dynamics of the primary motives or primary emotions. My strongest regret is that I have not been able to indicate explicitly the influence of contemporary psychological scholars whose work has helped me avoid stumbling more than I have.

A book that one has been writing all his academic life owes so much to his teachers, colleagues, students--even typists--who have been generous with their gifts. They remain unnamed but not forgotten. I cannot but acknowledge the good fortune for the aid, especially on psychological matters, of Professors Gordon W. Allport, R. Freed Bales, Abraham H. Maslow, and Thomas F. Pettigrew. To be urged on by such as Professor Brand Blanshard, Edwin A. Burtt, and Frederick R. Tennant, in addition to experiencing the support of Professor Edgar S. Brightman, my teacher and colleague, is good fortune indeed!

A Guggenheim Fellowship enabled me to spend most of the year 1960-1961 at King's College, University of London, where H. D. Lewis went more than the second mile in helping me to clarify persistent issues about the nature of the self. I am grateful to the Rockefeller Foundation for allowing me to spend a month at the Villa Serbelloni at Bellagio, and to the Boston University Graduate School for opportune aid.

My brother, Angelo P. Bertocci, has once more kept me from stylistic blunders and conceptual errors. Had the commitment, far beyond duty, of Ronald L. Carter, Dean of Students at Boston University, not been allied with that of my patiently courageous wife, this venture would never have come this far. Would that this work could be a worthy tribute to the efforts of so many over the years.

                                        Peter A. Bertocci

CONTENTS

CHAPTER ONE

The Person As a Unified Agent

A.   The person as conscious agent

1. The consciousness that persons have of themselves, their
capacity   for   self-awareness   or   self-consciousness,
distinguishes them from all other living beings including
those that are most like them. Whatever the scope and
limits of consciousness and self-consciousness may be, only
the self-conscious being can know them as he inspects his
activities, differentiates them, and relates them to each
other and to any beings-events other than themselves.

2. There is nothing in these statements that precludes any
specific view of the nature of the scope of conscious and
self-conscious knowing. Indeed, none of us remains long
unaware of the difficulties of inspecting his own

consciousness without seeking other avenues to trustworthy reports about its nature. The eminent psychologist of personality, Gordon W. Allport, mindful of the difficulties of validating claims made on the basis of immediate or direct experience, was not given to underrating the importance of publicly verifiable, objective evidence. Nevertheless, he emphasized that "the core of the objective method is still the reliance each scientist places upon the testimony of his own fugitive and overlapping conscious states. He can work with the Unconscious or with Bodily Constitution only as they are distilled into his own consciousness".[1]

3. Since so much in this book depends on the inspection and interpretation of conscious experience, it will be well to face the question: Is there direct conscious experience that is "innocent" of the interpretation that selects and relates experiences to other (interpreted) experiences? My basic reply: If there is a "neat," uninterpreted experience, it would be that of an infant who for the first time sees, or tastes, or smells, qualities, say, that he will later learn to "identify" as orange juice, and this owing to the fact that they do appear together despite changes in context. Thus, the problem that stalks each of us as knowers is to differentiate what is given (experience) and what is taken (interpreted experience).

But if the <u>givens</u> depend for their existence solely on interpretation, we have nothing to rely upon to guide us as we seek to understand the interpretations we give and to evaluate their relation to the problem at hand. One interpretation may be more inclusive than another, but sooner or later the verdict will depend upon that experience, or those experiences, that are "obstinately there" to support the interpretation: the interpretation "orange juice" is more dependably rooted in certain qualities directly experienced than is the interpretation "milk." In short, we find ourselves relying on given experiences, as warrant for this or that interpretation more than for any other. Hence, when we say that this interpretation (or hypothesis) is more adequate to experience than another, we are assuming that what is experienced has been inspected for what it is as given and "stands by" the interpretation more dependably.

Let this suffice to alert us to the larger context that needs attention as persons contrast their interpretations of experience "with experience itself" in their search for truth. What criterion of truth is the most trustworthy test of the truth-claims based on experience? I set out the criterion that keeps on recommending itself to me.

B.   The criterion of truth

1. If indeed what the truth-seeker experiences is necessary to any adequate account of himself and of his relation to his environment, he will grant no arbitrary priority to any experience as the source of truth. Even a truth-claim "based upon my undeniable experience" comes before competing claims in the court of self-conscious reasoning. Reasoning is the person acting, acting to weave together the different varieties of experiences, with a view to discovering which interpretation of them as a whole leaves the least data, relevant to the problem at hand, yet to be explained.

2. This reasoning, intent on the most systematic organization based on experience, never suspends the demands of logical consistency (or logical coherence), for the thinker cannot "digest" inconsistency as such between judgments. Assuming logical consistency in his reasoning, the truth-seeker is aiming at the most coherent interpretation of his experiences. His ideal of truth may well be called the criterion of experiential coherence-- indeed, of growing experiential coherence, since hitherto neglected or unknown evidence remains to be related to the hypothesis so far constructed. In sum, the criterion of growing experiential coherence guides the truth-seeker to that hypothesis which better than any other organizes the experiences and interpretations more coherently (or more

reasonably).

Hence, <u>reasonable</u> <u>probability</u>, more comprehensive than statistical probability, is the more <u>adequate</u> as the human test for truth. It can legitimately leave no stone of experience unturned, nor dismiss any relevant challenge to existing verdicts. In this sense, the more reasonably probable hypothesis is <u>more</u> <u>accurate</u> for the whole human venture in knowing and acting than is the accuracy that is achieved by applying methods and standards that, however successful in some areas of experience and interpretation, rather arbitrarily limit what is to be counted as evidence to begin with.

C.   The person's will-agency and will-power

1. It is not without cause that I focus on a very controversial dimension of the person as knowing agent, for without it, I suggest, the person reasoning would not be capable of guiding himself by his ideal of truth even. I am referring to will-agency, or free-will. The quality of purpos<u>ive</u> activity that a person undergoes as a feeling -wanting agent must be differentiated from the quality of purpose<u>ful</u> experience whereby he organizes his feelings and wants in accordance with some consciously held goal. In many situations the person allows the strongest feelings and

desires to "resolve" his conflicts. But in many other situations, when, say, the unapproved desire would predominate if the situation were left to resolve itself, the person experiences himself as free to exert himself in favor of his approved alternative. This experience of effort, this _fiat_, to borrow William James' term, as experienced, is undeniable; it too is as given as red, or as anger. This is not to say that this _fiat_ requires no interpretation, but it does mean that interpretation of this experience should not be imposed on it from other realms, neglecting the quality of the experience itself.

2. It is, however, one thing to hold that the person wills a goal, but another to say that his willing can achieve the goal. We must distinguish, therefore, the person's _will-agency_ from the actual power of willing (_will-power_). This distinction is tied to the fact that the willing person, given impediments in the situation within and beyond him, may be less effective than he anticipated. He does not deny that he experiences agency, but he becomes aware that he misjudged his actual power. Thus, while willing is an undeniable, constitutive activity of the person, his will-power derives from the actual interplay of the factors involved at choice-point. Some opponents of will-agency fear the horrendous result they (needlessly) anticipate if free-will is granted, namely, that a person could then capriciously create chaos in his experience. But this

opposition neglects the fact that will-agency does not occur within a vacuum, that the person at choice-point confronts habits, attitudes, traits within his acquired nature (as well as other constitutive factors in his nature) as he interacts with his environment.

3. Even were this distinction of will-agency and will-power completely erroneous, the hypothesis that the person in fact has no freedom to will among alternatives does have consequences even more horrendous than the alleged caprice that free-will would introduce into human experience. For if a person's experience and behavior are always the outcome of events that, from within and beyond him, converge upon him at any moment, the pursuit and achievement of true conclusions becomes impossible. For once we hold that true conclusions are outcomes of the dominant factors at work in a person at a given point, the truth-outcome is no different from the outcome of the interplay in any other complex or "competing" forces at hand.

But a person's claim that a certain conclusion is true rests on the assumption that he has been able to guide his search by his ideal of truth. For example, as I interpret the evidence relevant to a problem, presumably I have been able to resist the clamor of desire and the press of factors within me and beyond me as I try to draw the conclusion justified by the evidence. Note: if I have no will-agency at all, even to will the continuance of thinking (when my desire favors giving up), or if I have no will-agency to forgo a conclusion, or to postpone it until I am convinced that it is the one best related to the evidence at hand, then how can I possibly claim that my conclusion is true (and not the sheer outcome of events that left me no choice)? Hence, to the indubitable awareness of will-agency, I have added a theoretical consideration without which it means nothing to say that a conclusion is true.

D.   The essence of the person

1. I turn from these capacities, essential for the person as purposeful knower, to the nature of the person's unity and continuity. In passing, I must grant that I cannot of course legislate the substitution of the word person for such words as soul, self, spirit, mind, psyche. But minimally I intend a self-conscious being capable of criticizing "his" experiences, his conscious undergoings, by reasonable norms. Such qualifications as male, female, homosexual, and others, are important to a person's life-history (or personality). But when person dominates my reference it is this capacity to be not only conscious but also self-conscious that is necessary to his search for reasonable conclusions that are of the essence. 2. But I must face the question: What is comprehended in consciousness and self-consciousness? I cannot but assume

that consciousness is an ultimate in the sense that there is no going beyond it to explain it. We cannot find something, consciousness, independent of the activities that distinguish us whenever we are conscious in any manner. It is these activities and their potential that define consciousness-selfconsciousness. Without assuming that these differentiations are final or complete, I propose that a person is aware of himself as the complex unity of activity-potentials: sensing, remembering, imagining, thinking, feeling, emoting, wanting, willing, oughting, and activities of aesthetic and religious appreciation. These activity-potentials--however finally interpreted--are to be conceived not as levels but as dimensions of a person; they constitute the experiential phases of a person's consciousness and self-consciousness. The inevitable question arises: How shall we interpret the fact that these activities seem to be different ways in which one being is and expresses himself? I shall write in the first-person as I present the experiential grounds that are basic to the interpretation that I advocate.

E. The person as a self-identifying unity

1. I am engaged in seeking truth and realizing ideals. These activities inherently involve changes related to actualizing or realizing goal(s). Yet I, the acting seeker

and the realizer, am both the same and different. For example, as I make any statement or proposal, I experience changes as I think different thoughts and as I try to express them. I undergo a succession of experiencings and "objects" of experiencing.

My first concern is to give some account of these changes of experiences that are successive. Succession is no phase of any change as such. Hence, as Borden P. Bowne[2] would say, a succession of experiences is not the experience of succession. For succession to be succession, and not substitution, there must be a continuant that in some way co-exists with that succession. But even this wording can beguile me into thinking that there are two things: the continuant and the succession. In order for me to know that Big Ben is striking the tenth time, I must have been aware of the first stroke and continued to be aware as I discriminate the next nine strokes as a succession. Had I changed completely as each stroke followed the other, I would not know that succession had taken place.[3]

2. If this conclusion seems inescapable, the conception of the continuant unity--I, self, person--is not. Before defending it, I present the view that recommends itself to me. If no judgment, be it logical, factual, or evaluative, can be thought without succession "in" the proposing experient, then it is because I, the proposer, am present at the beginning and end of each judgment, and this without my

being "exhausted in," or "absorbed by," or "arrested in," any stage of judgment-making. As the experient thus involved in each "successive" stage of proposing, I am a self-identifying being, that is, a unity in change who continues in and through the changes I am undergoing. I am a unity not because of a purpose I develop; I am a unity of activities to begin with. But what can it mean to say that a being is both one and many at the same time, or both identical and different at the same time?

3. That change--as opposed to substitution--involves continuity is clear; even a substitution, as when one teaches for another, involves some continuity of function. I find it, therefore, not the least surprising that great thinkers have insisted that changing is understandable only as an expression of something identical or unchanging. Yet, if I say that _my_ changing involves something unchanging, or literally identical, I find my actual experiencing at odds with this assertion. The only way I can capture in words what I am undergoing is to suggest that identity and unity are not to be understood as identity and unity in the logical or mathematical sense. That A is A, 2=2, exemplifies what I mean by mathematical or logical identity. Yet, as I say, I cannot find this _kind_ of identity in the experiencing I undergo as I think or utter these sentences.

I conclude: the "sameness" that makes possible any defining of the "identity" that must be maintained if there is to be any experiencing even of any proposition, is never sameness or identity in a logical sense. Therefore, I prefer the word self-identifying for the kind of unity and sameness that I experience. To be sure, I still hear echoes of much historical discussion to the effect that there cannot be similarity without sameness. But I must simply submit that clear as logical sameness, identity, and equality are to me as ideas, I find no referent for them in the matter-of-fact world, or in my experiencing.

4. For me to say that I am I is to say that I am aware of myself as continuous in any now, and as continuing in and through similar and yet different nows in more inclusive nows. This kind of experiencing I hold to be the primordial or primitive given.

It should be clear that I am not using the word experiencing as the foundation for any specific epistemological or metaphysical contention about what I experience; I mean it in the primitive sense--though open to further interpretation--as stipulating what it means concretely to be conscious. I use the present participle "experiencing" to suggest that being conscious is never sheer passivity, whatever the "object" or "objective" of experiencing may finally turn out to be. In short, to be a person is to be at least conscious, to undergo, as a unity -continuity, the distinctive kinds of activities that constitute that matrix of unity-continuity.

5. There is one specific consequence I find it reasonable to draw immediately. There is no I, no self, no soul, no mind, no consciousness, that is in any way separate from, or distinct from, these activities and their potentials. As a person I am a complex unity of experiencing; I am a sensing, remembering, perceiving, thinking, feeling, emoting, oughting, willing, and appreciating being (including aesthetic and religious experiencing). I am not (as Descartes, Locke, Berkeley, and even Kant, each in his way, held), a "that which" thinks, and so on. There are not states or modes of consciousness being that need to be unified or made into a subject of experiencing. There is not an I that has, rather than is, its varied experiencing or activities.

This notion of the self-identifying unity-in-continuity is proposed as a more reasonable alternative to a great historic thesis that some identical unity is needed as the unchanging ground for continuity in succession. But my alternative requires more defense, especially since it turns its back also on the historic counter-proposal that the personal self cannot but be a bundle or a collection of experiencings and experienceds--as held by Hume and his followers, and, for different motives, by many in Buddhist philosophy. The self-identifying person is neither a collection of experiences, a gradually developed construction "from experiences," nor even, as some process philosophers suggest, the result of a route of experiences.

F. The self-identifying person as primordial unity

1. In defense of what must seem an arbitrary stipulation of a primordial fact of experience, self-identifying unity-in -continuity, I shall expand my proposal with serious objections in mind.

"You have urged," it may well be objected, "that the succession intrinsic to such experiencings (activity -potentials, such as thinking or sensing), involves a unity -continuity that is never exhausted in any one activity and yet never transcends the activities that constitute it. You therefore characterize this unity as a unity of these activities, and regard the activities as the essential referent of the word I. You claim that the notion of I -continuity must not be assimilated to that of logical identity. But are you appealing to some intuitive knowledge of self to support this conclusion that there is neither the existence nor the knowledge of succession in experiencing without a continuant-I? You oppose our direct inspection, for example, to that of Hume who said that when he looked into himself he could never find any unity, or more than fleeting sensations and feelings. How do you support your view?"

My answer is that I cannot support it in the sense that I can prove that this particular view of I follows from some premise. The I to which I am pointing does not loom up as some specific qualitative entity in some way distinct from any or all of its activities. I would say that this I-unity is being stipulated were I not trying to say that it is definable only as these distinguishable activity-potentials. (Obviously, that there are these irreducible activity-potentials needs to be granted me at this point, but my main thesis does not depend on how many there are.) I use the word "intuitive" for my knowing myself, not to suggest that I am directly aware of some being distinct from the matrix of activities I am calling I. In asserting, therefore, that I have intuitive knowledge I am suggesting that I is not the conclusion of some line of reasoning. Accordingly, in my situation, I must be satisfied with no more than the comment: my experiencing of myself as self-identifying unity-continuity is like no other situation because what we might speak of as the object of awareness is simply not an object among objects, not an activity among activities, at all; without it, as complex unity of activities, there would be no "objects" or "objectives" or activity-potentials.

2. If these affirmations seem to presuppose excessive confidence in the inspection of experiencing, I can only point out, methodologically, that he who claims that I am mistaken must be appealing to his own inspection, or direct awareness, to support his objection. I do not know how he can say that my analysis is correct or incorrect unless he can "know" his experiences as I claim I am knowing mine. I can only invite him to check my description-interpretation by his; but neither of us can avoid the fact that, in proposing descriptions-interpretations, we are self-conscious, and that we are the-same-and-different proponents at every stage in the affirming-process. I am urging that the affirming agent is--whatever else--a unity-continuity who knows himself in a way unlike his knowing of anything else. Again, the experient in all knowing does not "know" himself, or "experience" himself, in the same way as he distinguishes any aspect of himself or any "object" other than himself. And I add, for the moment, that I experience, _and_ _in_ _this_ _instance_ _know_, myself in a way best expressed by the words, _self_-_identifying_ _unity_-_continuity_.

Reflection on this puzzling matter makes me more sympathetic with Berkeley's contention that he never knew himself via ideas but that he had a "notion" of himself. Berkeley's particular view of ideas as passive made it all the more difficult for him to say that he knew himself as an active being via passive ideas. His basic difficulty,

nevertheless, is instructive; I do not know myself (as I),
as I know a process or an event, or an entity, or an idea,
or a quality. H. H. Price has said: "Matters of fact can
only be known by experience; and experience must always be
the experience of some individual conscious being. It has
to be first-hand if it is to exist at all. But when one
individual learns about the experiences of others, he can
only do so by his own first-hand experience of the words he
hears or sees."4 I paraphrase: I, as conscious unity
-continuity of activities, is given as involved in all
specific experiencings but never known as any of them is
known. The light, by which we see all that needs light in
order to be seen, is not itself known as any lighted objects
are known.

3. I must make unmistakable what I do not assert at this
stage of analysis. I am not justified in claiming any
particular theory of mind or body, or relation between them.
What I am claiming may be troublesome to anyone who already
believes that the human mind is the brain, or that it is a
center of God's being. Neither view is shut out at this
point, though I shall hold that both are unreasonable
interpretations of the data of consciousness. But I may say
here that I cannot accept the view, so often made the
foundation for proposals on this issue, that we do somehow
already have fairly definitive knowledge of what "body"
means. The contention I am defending, and shall explain

further, is that I, whatever else we come to say about it, is most reasonably interpreted as a self-identifying unity -in-continuity of conscious activity-potentials, and that what we can accept as "body" must be coherent with what we find in that conscious experience. If this continuant -unity, that alone makes the experience of succession intelligible, can later be defined as instantiations of bodily (or divine) being, we shall need to change our view. But such contentions are far from evident, and the case must be made rather than assumed, be it on scientific or on religious grounds.

4. Nor am I saying that the mere fact that I say that I intuit myself as being x or y makes it finally coherent. No act of intuitive awareness tells us all we wish to know. I am claiming at the outset, nevertheless, that I as self -experiencing is given in a way that nothing else is given, and that the closest description-interpretation of I is a unity-continuity of activities that I discern as distinguishable but not separate.

Accordingly, every statement I make about I-awareness or I-consciousness is open to further examination. I cannot say that I have adequate knowledge about myself until I have satisfied myself not only that my description-interpretation does capture what is taking place "as" my experience, but also that it is more reasonable than other proposals that can be made with reason about me. In a word, any theory of

I, proposed by an I, must depend on self-awareness and the experiencings that define it, without assuming that any data thus experienced are the only considerations involved in the I's full being or in its search for truth.

Still, why not exclude self-awareness of I in this restricted sense, since it is interpretative? My answer is, "I cannot even if I would. For I do not even know how I can correct an interpretation except on the basis of self -awareness and the data provided therewith and therein." I am asserting, in other words, what H. H. Price terms an "inspectively-evident proposition," without asserting that I know with inspective assurance that I am correct about any theory I give regarding the unity and continuity, for example, of my awareness.[5] Others can help me only on the basis of what they find in their self-awareness. Since I cannot in fact dispose of interpretation, I can only reassert the view which makes the very possibility of interpretation most reasonable: I am a continuant-unity without which "self-identifying" is impossible. This I is not an object like other objects, such as the objects of perceiving, remembering, thinking, and so on. I am this particular unified matrix of activities that define me as the continuant of activities. But further elaboration of what "continuant" involves is now required.

G.   The nature of the datum person

1. Let us consider any _erlebt_ present (or experiencing _now_).
I begin with this _erlebt_ present because, whatever else
exists, in the environment or in other (inferred) aspects of
my nature, I can never deny this experiencing present. It
is the home base for any excursion I make; I am experiencing
always "in" or "as" a _now_--as opposed to "then" and "not
-yet." What I discriminate as the activities of feeling,
emoting, wanting, willing, oughting, sensing, remembering,
thinking, and appreciating are always unified "in" a now.
(I shall often use the terms "knowing-wanting self or
person", or "agent-person" as shorthand for this complex
matrix of activities or experiencings. This telescoping of
activities is not intended to annul distinctions between
each as discerned--for example, the difference between
willing, remembering, and wanting, or between logical
cognition and perceptual cognition.)

Any present awareness, then, is a unity of the knowing
-wanting activities which are that complex person. There is
not awareness or consciousness _plus_ these activities. To be
conscious is to be aware in these ways, each needing
description and interpretation; to be a _now_ of consciousness
is to be knowing-wanting to some degree. My now is my _now_
in the sense that only as a now am I able to _remember_ some

experiences in contrast to those that I <u>anticipate</u> in a now.

Edgar S. Brightman (1884-1953) calls this slice of personal experience both "the datum self," and "the shining present." Brightman refers to it as "the source of evidence," as "the immediacy of feeling," and says it "contains all presently observable consciousness--all sensations, images, reasoning, loves, hates, fears, and hopes of now, all conations, strivings and efforts, desires, aversions."[6] There is a similar emphasis on the "interpretation" of activities as a present unity in A. N. Whitehead`s passage: "Descartes' `Cogito, ergo sum' is wrongly translated, `I <u>think</u>, therefore I am.' It is never bare thought or bare existence that we are aware of. I find myself essentially a unity of emotions, enjoyments, hopes, fears, regrets, valuations of alternatives, decisions--all of them subjective reactions to the environment as active in my nature. My unity--which is Descartes' `I am'--is my process of shaping this welter of material into a consistent pattern of feelings."[7] Agreed, with the proviso that there must be a primitive unity of these knowing-wanting activities that acts to shape the <u>acquired</u> unity resulting from its interaction with the environment. For, again, whatever else "existence" may include or involve, I cannot get away from this <u>erlebt</u>, complex matrix of activities as a <u>given</u>, <u>initial</u>, <u>irreducible</u> <u>unity</u>. In Cartesian terms, to deny it is to assert it. But what is deniable is the Cartesian _view_ that `Cogito' presupposes the unity of soul -substance that exists unchanged from moment to moment. What is undeniable is this "saddle-back" _now_ (not a mathematical instant), the _durée_ of its complex unity. Whatever else is or is not reasonable to deny, I cannot deny the experiencing _now_.

Not simply in passing, however, we should note that Descartes did not define his Cogito as sheer intellectual unity. A thinking thing, he said in the Second Meditation, is a "thing which doubts, understands, conceives, affirms, denies, wills, refuses, which also imagines and feels." That existentialists, of all thinkers, should have neglected this elaboration, adds to the segmental interpretations from which Descartes has suffered.[8]

2. Hence, while I cannot deny without affirming the datum person, I must leave to reasonable inference the questions about its relation to other things, including the body, for example. As I see it, when John Maynard Smith, Professor of Zoology, University of Sussex, says: "The two statements, `I have a sensation of blueness' and `there is a particular pattern of physical events in my brain,' are descriptions of different aspects of the same event,"[9] he seems to overlook the fact that what the neurological activity associated with the experience of blueness is a scientific inference that is not as certain as the experience of blue. Descartes was

correct at one point: whatever other realities we may believe in, "thinking" activities constitute a matrix that is reaffirmed with every attempt at denial. I cannot, as I have said, follow him in the theory that only an unchanging unity can unite successive experiences.

How, then, do I get beyond the datum person or beyond this "solipsism of the present moment," to use Santayana's phrase? Not simply by asserting that I do! There are no proofs here, but there is an interpretation that coheres with what is experienced by the datum person. We must remember that, in any now, reasoning occurs, and asks questions about what seems clearly to be given in, and to, the present experiencing. For example: what causes some of my refractory experiences and their refractory order? Were they my own creation, I probably could alter them. A reasoning datum person will infer that there are other existents constraining and influencing the nature and course of his development. In short his constant task is to develop reasonable hypotheses about himself in relation to the environment with which he interacts. But he cannot assume, to begin with, any particular view of that environment. An adequate epistemology is called for here. But my present concern is only to deny the kind of argument that seems to go: "Because solipsism is `unbelievable,' we must begin with [what turns out to be a particular view of] the existent world." (In the future I shall capitalize, as

in Environment and World or Object, what is <u>inferred</u> as
other than experient, and open to other interpretations--as
opposed to what we in common sense, or under other
presumably direct conditions, refer to as <u>e</u>nvironment,
<u>w</u>orld, <u>o</u>bject.)

3. I pass, then, to a basic question: How does the datum
person move from his <u>now</u> to knowledge of the past? How do I
know my past? On what grounds do I affirm my past? My main
answer: Some experiences in my <u>now</u> have a given "again"
quality about them. Obviously, what is involved here is not
simply the validity of memory but why we even assert that we
remember. Without such "agains" in a datum person, there is
no experiential base of <u>remembering</u>. Note: I may be wrong
about my interpretation of <u>what</u> I am <u>now</u> experiencing <u>again</u>.
This color that I am experiencing as red-again may not be
that of the apple I saw this morning, or this anger-again
that I now experience may not be directed at the same object
I experienced this morning; the inference may be wrong, but
the experienced "again" is undeniable. In short, I assert
with H. H. Price,[10] that anything I experience as "again"
is as undeniable as my experience of the color red. But
such experiences may be interpreted incorrectly. In other
words, I would not know "the past," as the past, were there
no experience of "again" "in" the datum person. How the
datum person interprets himself in the light of this
experience of "again" is another matter, but it will

presuppose his experience of "again" in a <u>now</u>.

To generalize: All objects of my experience I always experience "in" my now-matrix; and this includes reference to my "past experience." <u>What</u> I find reasonable <u>to</u> <u>conclude</u> about my past is the most coherent hypothesis based on my varied experiences of "again" and on other relevant evidence. For sheer experiences of recognition are no proof that I am correct in particular judgments about what I recognize. Again-ness is no inference, but all particular memorial judgments, and all other judgments involving the past, depend ultimately on given evidence of pastness. Thus, I may be wrong about a specific judgment I make about myself "in the past," but were there no given experience, in a now, of "me again," I would have no basis for talking about remembering, and no basis for the hypothesis about my nature as a now-being who remembers.

The metaphysical interpretation of this given datum person is not in discussion now. Yet, once more, this much is basic: did I not have the experience of "me-again," there would be no experiential basis of asserting that I am the same, self-<u>identifying</u> person I was when I started writing this page. Whatever mistake I may make as I try to interpret <u>what</u> makes such continuity possible, there would be no experiential base for any judgment about continuity were I not a self-identifying person who is able to reason, on the basis of again-experiences, about my relation to all other data, present, retained, and recalled.

H. The nature of the continuant person

1. Let us return to this problem of explaining continuity. It is tempting to consider personal continuity as that of an identical, unchanging soul-substance,[11] that is, a "pure" ego or subject, involved in cognitive and other activities, without which they would not be united, but never itself revealed in any of them. This "thread" unifying the "beads" of experience, to use a resisted analogy, has been criticized in different ways by James, Bergson, Royce, Whitehead, Hartshorne, Brightman, and others. The soul -person, as these critics urge, cannot be a changeless being and be immanent in the changing experiences that are _its_ own. Furthermore, even within the dynamics of a lived _now_ there is some continuity-unity before a new _now_ is born: "I am feeling angry now, but angrier than I was." "The colors of the sunset that I am seeing now are noticeably darker than they were a moment ago." As the colors as I experienced them are gone, so also is my self of _that_ experience. If I cannot think of these moments of new-experience as expressive of a soul-substance, which somehow spans and integrates successive moments within its own being, can I suggest a more adequate interpretation of the

continuity within and "between" nows?

2. What follows presupposes and elaborates two points, already mentioned. First, it is only within my now that any being-becoming takes place; there is no "between" nows. It is as this active now that I experience differences. The differences are not separations; they are distinctions within the total complex unity that I am calling the datum person. It is this experiencing-now that I present as the undeniable unity without which the words "experiencing" and "experiences" become meaningless.

Second, given this unity, we must be extremely careful in conceiving how it is possible for continuity "between" nows to be. We must not be misled by the spatial images of our language, in this case by "between" or "among" nows, as if there were an intervening link or bridge between nows and what we experience. "Ingestion" and "digestion" go on "in" a datum person. Something from "within" always ceases to be even as its experience becomes more complex. For it is "in" that now that there is remembering, reasoning, sensing, wanting (and so on), and it is "in" that now that we find the grounds for any "has been" and any "not-yet".

3. Here I would dwell further on H. H. Price's view of recognition. "Again-ness" is, as he says, as much given to me as the color red is given me. It is understood that "again" is not given as such, but only as a "quality" of

experience--for instance, as "red-again." I may not want this red that I recognize any more than I want this or that feeling. It is this refractory nature of the "recognitive -object," if I may so call it, that opens the way for my reasonable assurance (not proof) that my now gives evidence of a beyond my now that is somehow related to my now.

In short, I seem to be the kind of being that as a now am somehow connected with a past, with a no-longer, even as I change and identify myself. I can be mistaken about my interpretation of what I remember just as I can give more than one, and possibly mistaken, interpretation of the other "objective" presentations (colors, sounds, and so on) that I undeniably experience. Yet, without "recognitive objects" within my growing-changing-dying now, I would have no ground for believing in my past. No recognitive experience, then no hint of my past; and such again-experiences are the basis for my interpretation of my history as a person.

I. The unity-continuity of the person, and memory

1. A particular interpretation of memory is being suggested here. I bring this chapter to a close by suggesting a way of conceiving a personal unity that helps to understand the possibility of remembering what no longer exists.[12]

I have said: It is I-now who remembers, but what I remember, I remember on the basis of "again-ness" in my now.

This I-now, is somehow related to my then. But how shall I conceive of the peculiar continuity that exists between my now, always present, and my no longer nows? We probably cannot get away from pictorial, spatializing models of successive identity, but I find singularly inadequate the view advanced by A. N. Whitehead and his followers generally. This "linear view" of continuity emphasizes that the unity of the person is essentially a passage of the past into the selective present unity. But I ask, what concretely can it mean to say that I, at present moment b, am what I am because of what a no-longer existent moment, a, has passed on to me? This spatial picture will not do. For how, on this view, can a (present) be or know b that as past is gone? Some bridge c, that is neither a nor b but a bridge, is required, and this no matter how narrow the span. And so on ad infinitum. What seems to be continuity is in fact not forthcoming on such a view, for one a (past) cannot pass itself on to a b (now) that is not yet existent. Retrospectively, this linear view seems to make sense, but only because the continuity is assumed rather than explained.

2. I suggest as a more adequate model that the datum person a does not "move" to b (not-yet). A never "passes" itself on, partially or wholly. Rather is the datum person a unity of activities that undergoes its change, maintains its self-identity in its changes from a to b. The successor to a is

not b; a is itself, succeeds itself, as the b. B is what a was with its potential for b. Datum person a, responding selectively to the Environment pressing upon it, does that which its capacities for wanting-knowing allow in each situation. This means that datum person a at b is datum person a, still itself, yet in a new way. The future of a, namely b, is a, the "womb" of b's becoming. This "pregnant" datum person, this a-matrix is both different and the same as it becomes b, that is, as it selectively shapes itself in response to its world.

To restate the same conception dynamically: some developments within me (within me as a datum person), and some interactions with the Environment, can threaten my very being-becoming. But if a datum person can be-come or continue to be-come at all, it is a become b. Thus datum person b is what datum person a became, having survived the possibly "threatening" and possibly "nourishing" environment. More familiarly, as b I am aware of myself as a "again," and also as a new a to some extent. But I (datum person) at a cannot pass my identity on to b since it is not-yet! Nor have I, as a, remained myself by "reaching back" into a past--existent no longer!--in order to maintain myself. In short, recognition at my moment b is possible because b is I (datum person) altered, and yet not a stranger. Memory, or I-remembering-a, is possible only because a maintains its identity in becoming-being b, namely, a in a new-yet-old stage. Time thus marches on as a, enduring now, finds itself capable of remaining itself with its difference (as is evidenced by its knowing, at b, that it is itself altered but not "alienated" from a).

3. Similarly, my future is not the offspring of my present which dies in the future. My future is my present, changed, enriched, growing, decaying, but never so much as to lose its intrinsic act-ive and selective unity. A spatial image will not do: but if a mobile could grow, it might help as a pictorial model. For a mobile keeps its basic structure even though it "yields," here and there, in response to its own inner dynamic in a changing environment.

Accordingly, the person-mobile can remember (can retain, recognize, and recall) because it is always a present-self -identifying with its past and shaping its future; that is, it has been able to persist as active unity even as it changed and developed, and this both in accordance with demands of its own nature and in interaction with its total Environment.

4. Such a view can perhaps win credence only with the aid of a shift in our way of thinking about memory. My suggestion so far is that remembering is possible because (barring death or complete decay) we never do lose our basic continuity as a unity of activities. From our very birth, as active unities, we are able, in interaction with our total Environment, to maintain and develop our unity-in

-continuity as we undergo change. We cannot explain such "sameness" by imagining a past, a no-longer, passing into a non-existent future. Remembering is an activity of the datum person that exists always and only as a present that endures through its own inner complexity in selective response to its ambient. Thus, a person, in remembering, is ever a present; as he experiences again-ness within his present, he seeks to connect this again-ness with other available data. The experiencing of retention, the actual occurrence of self-identifying (as in recognition and recall), testify, I suggest, to a kind of being-becoming whose succession calls (in a non-linear, non-spatial model) for a self-identifying experient, the person.

5. I shall now describe this model of the datum-and-continuant-person in a way that may suggest more clearly both the cross-sectional unity and the horizontal continuity. At cross-section: a person is a unity of wanting-knowing activities which exist always as an undeniable, irreducible, now. Thus, in any now, a person is wanting, he is remembering, he is thinking... At any moment he is "on the go," wanting and aiming, now knowing how far he can satisfy his wants, not knowing exactly what his sensory and memorial (and other data) involve. As Luce puts it, Berkeley described his I, mind, as "the concrete of the will and understanding,"[13] in order to emphasize the unity and the activity in the complex unity of his being.

This cross-sectional moment of personal being-becoming needs to be supplemented by the horizontal (successive) view. For a person, we have said, is able to be a self-identifying unity-continuity. Once created, he is able to alter and maintain himself, in accordance with his "posited" nature, as he sustains himself in relation to the Environment. The experience of "again," and other memorial activities, are our evidence for this maintaining-sustaining that we call "retaining." However, we must stop thinking of the past and future as if they were railway tracks over which our train has passed as it moves onto the track further ahead. The past is always a present memory, cognitively; and ontically it is always at least a phase and factor of a present that is what it is because of the way it has selectively dealt with all of its experiences. Yet some experiences are forgotten; they cease to be.[14]

This last remark needs comment. It is often said that one never really forgets anything. But for this reservoir-theory of the past (not to say dump-heap theory) I can see no actual evidence. Have I not forgotten, once and for all, the many streetcars and other places I have been in, the many numbers of hotel rooms I was careful to remember at the time, the quantities of marbles won or lost when I was seven years old? One could give thousands of examples. To speak as if there were a kind of law of the conservation of mental energy is simply to prove once more how prone we are to carry into the psychic world ways of thinking that seem established in the physical. Were we to carry all of our past with us, our psychic unity might well be overcome. Obviously, it must remain an empirical question how much a given person does retain and can recall, given the proper stimulus and conditions. But it is time to emphasize that "going out of being" in the psychic realm seems to be a fact about mental experience which we must admit rather than eliminate.

J.   Reflective overview

The upshot of our consideration may be put thus: A person, or personal self, is essentially a complex unity of activities capable of interacting with the impinging Environment without losing that unity. A person, as long as he exists, maintains his self-identity as he selectively interacts with his Environment, and develops, conserves, and loses his potential; that is, he does not simply "continue to be." This is a way of specifying: to be, for a person, is to act or be acted upon.

But it is to say more. To be a person is to be that quality of being-becoming that is, within limits, self -renewing and self-destructive at any particular stage of being-becoming. A person is no route of nows; one is tempted to say, he is a now forever actively en route--

until...? But then one remembers those stoppages en route --short of death--namely, the discontinuities and the intermissions that at once seem to break up and to sustain the kind of unity-continuity the person is. Accordingly, the view so far presented is incomplete, indeed, inadequate if such discontinuities cannot be accommodated by it better than on other views.

Notes for Chapter One

1.   Gordon   W.   Allport,   Personality: A   Psychological
Interpretation (New York: Holt, 1937), 159.

2.   Borden P. Bowne (1864-1910) may be called the founder of
      American Personalistic Idealism. His basic books are
Theory of Thought and Knowledge (1897) and Metaphysics (1882) rev.
ed. 1898.

3.   I owe this illustration to C. A. Campbell. See his
Selfhood and Godhood (London: Allen and Unwin), 1957).

4.   H. H. Price, "Retrospect," in Biology and Personality:
      Frontier Problems in Science, Philosophy and Religion,
ed. Ian T. Ramsey (Oxford: Blackwell, 1965), 208. In the same
volume see the chapters by John Maynard Smith and Ian Ramsey. See
also P. F. Strawson, Individuals (London: Methuen and Co.,
1959), 89 and 94ff.

5.   H. H. Price, Belief (London: Allen and Unwin, 1969),
232ff.

6.   Edgar S. Brightman, Person and Reality, ed. Peter A.
Bertocci in collaboration with Jannette E. Newhall and Robert S.
Brightman (New York: Ronald Press, 1958), 35, 36. See also his A
Philosophy of Religion (New Jersey: Englewood Cliffs: Prentice
Hall, 1940); "The Finite Self," in Contemporary Idealism in

America, ed. Clifford Barrett (New York: Macmillan, 1932). I take this occasion to acknowledge a heavy debt to the teaching and writing of Edgar Sheffield Brightman.

7. Alfred N. Whitehead, Modes of Thought (New York: Macmillan, 1938), 227, 228.

8. Zeno Vendler in Res Cogitans: An Essay in Rational Psychology (New York: Cornell University Press, 1972), helps to bring needed balance at this critical point. I should still wish to insist that Descartes is defining incontrovertible existence as thinking, not vice-versa, as Vendler himself seems to hold (see 201 f.). My appreciation of Vendler's study is not decreased by his final decision that "both I's in I think and I exist refer to a transcendental I, the I that remains the same throughout my mental history."

9. From his essay, "An Agnostic View of Evolution," in Biology and Personality, ed. Ian T. Ramsey (Oxford: Blackwell, 1965), 58.

10. H. H. Price, Thinking and Experience (Cambridge: Harvard University Press, 1953).

11. The best defenses of this sort of view are to be found in the much too neglected work of F. R. Tennant, Philosophical Theology, 2 vols. (Cambridge: Cambridge University Press, 1928; 1970), and of H. D. Lewis, The Elusive Mind (London: Allen and Unwin, 1969). For a different perspective, see Paul Tillich,

Systematic Theology, vol. 1 and especially vol. 3 (Chicago: Chicago University Press, 1963). The works of E. L. Mascall, of which The Openness of Being (Philadelphia: Westminster Press, 1971) is an excellent, comprehensive expression, are lucid presentations of a Thomist non-temporalism.

12. See also my "A Temporalistic View of Personal Mind," Theories of Mind, ed. Gordon M. Scher (New York: The Free Press, 1962), 398-421; "Susan K. Langer's Theory of Feeling and Mind," Review of Metaphysics, 23 (March, 1970):527-551; "The Essence of a Person," Monist, 61 (Jan. 1978):28-41; "The Person, His Personality, and Environment," Review of Metaphysics, 32 (June, 1979):605-621.

13. A. A. Luce, The Dialectic of Immaterialism (London: Hodder and Stoughton, 1963), 174, 175.

14. For discussion of self-identity and memory see S. Shoemaker, Self-Knowledge and Self-Identity (Ithaca, New York: Cornell University Press, 1963), and H. D. Lewis, The Elusive Mind (London: Allen and Unwin, 1969), chapter 10, for a critique of this view. I may further remark that in H. D. Lewis' book, I find a most telling critique of recent attempts to define mind and its identity in relation to the body; for example, of Ryle, Hirst, Ayer, Strawson, J. C. C. Smart, and S. Shoemaker. Lewis' careful

study of opposing views is exemplary, and the development of his own treatment of "the elusive mind" is compelling. His critique expresses most of my concerns and I can only wish that I had his gift for description and positive construction. Some may find the interchange between H. D. Lewis and myself interesting: see Religious Studies, 15 (1979):399-408, "Does Elusive Becoming in Fact Characterize H. D. Lewis' View of the Mind?"

CHAPTER TWO

The Person and the Unconscious

A.   The   problem: unity   of   the   person   despite
intermittent consciousness

In this chapter I shall suggest the direction in which the
theory of the person I am proposing should be expanded,
especially in view of the phenomena of sleep and some
influential concepts of "the unconscious."
1. The complex unity-continuity of the datum person is, I have
argued, undeniable and irreducible. I shall pursue the thesis
that I could not identify myself as myself, as a continuant
unity from moment to moment, and also over intermittency, were
I not the kind of being who, in my present, does undergo again
-experiences. Any specific claim about what these experiences
mean is subject to the same criterion of truth as any other
claim, namely, to experiental coherence. For example, my
experience of "me-again" does not carry with it some indelible
postmark indicating the amount of time that has elapsed between

"me-now" and "me-then." I cannot infer with certainty from any experience of me-again that there is no lapse between my now and my "me just a moment ago" or just passing.[1]

We must keep these considerations in mind as we seek to interpret the specific continuity, despite intermittency, that we affirm as we awake from sleep. "I went to sleep `last night' and here I am this morning." In this situation none of us doubts psychologically that he went to sleep and after a period (whose length he may well misjudge) he awakens as "myself-again." Assuming that the psychological certitude of my being a unity-continuity can be reasonably supported along the lines proposed in the last chapter, the question we now face is: On this view, how shall unity-continuity during periods of suspended awareness, during intermittency without consciousness, be understood?

2. Any datum person has the task of maintaining his identity, given internal change and interactions with his ambient. "Maintaining his identity" means to persist as the self -identifying unity of his activity-potentials. The potentials do not exist independently of his activities, but they refer to the fact that any activity, not fully actual at any one moment, is ready to respond in this way or in another (within limits). Thus I sense this color but I can sense another also; I remember this event, but I could have remembered another; I am imagining the joy of an anticipated event, but I can imagine what may happen if it does not occur--and so on, for every

activity. Every datum person is at any moment never actually all he can be, although he may be doing all he can do at that moment. Accordingly, I propose: <u>The quality of identity-in -change of the unity-continuity that is a person, is no more and no less than his constitutive activities with their potentials. These activity-potentials mature and are modified by learning and thus predispose the person to some, rather than other, more specific responses to his ambient.</u> A potentiality is defined by the activity of which it is potential; there is no potentiality without actuality, as Aristotle reminded us. There is no telling in advance of experience what challenges or threats the activity-potentials of a person can endure and in what way. But, in thinking about change and continuity, we cannot get along without the concept of potentiality. We shall put this concept to more specific use as we interpret the data of intermittent consciousness.

3. Does the intermittency that we call sleep involve a particular form of potentiality that characterizes the kind of actuality that persons are? I am assuming that in deep sleep there is no consciousness in any sense in which we apply the word to our waking states. In deep sleep I am indeed both "dead to the world" and "dead" to myself. Note, I am not trying to save continuity by saying that even in dreamless sleep I am to some degree conscious. For I would be going beyond the evidence if I say, as is often said, that in dreamless sleep I am "really" still conscious. I am not, and

this constitutes a problem for my understanding the fact of my continuity after dreamless sleep. When I "awake" after such complete un-consciousness, I do know myself as the same-yet -different. Can I account for such phenomena on my view that bases continuity at every moment on the fact that any present is pregnant with its past, but doesn't "reach back" to a past?

4. It is at this point that I am tempted to become an epiphenomenalist and hold that psychic activity is a by-product of brain-events. I could then invoke the continuity of physiological processes in the body in order to bridge the periods between waking states, deep sleep, dreaming, and all the other states of sleep, such as fitful or restless sleep and drowsiness.

Yet such a solution is no solution, since it shifts the problem to that of continuity in cell-changes. The problems of ebb and flow are at least philosophically as great on the biological level as they are on the psychic level. The consolation provided by the thought: "My body was there in bed from 11:00 p.m. to 6:30 a.m. and it remained continuous in dreamless or deep sleep," is shortlived. The fact still is that I was tired, and without hope, when I went to bed; I am awake now, and hopeful. Certainly my brain-cells, or the ultimate constituents that compose them, have changed in the period between fatigue and refreshment. Why assume that they are the same-continuous "through" this intermittency? If we do, we face the same problem of continuity despite intermittency at this physiological level. Hence, I still am faced with the question: How, given this intermittent period of fatigue, can I say that this morning-body is identical with last-night's body?

5. So, with no relief from physiology, I still need to interpret the intermittency of consciousness on my view of the person. My waking from sleep, despite the discontinuity of consciousness, is called _my_ waking because in the moment of waking I recognize myself as "me-again" (as same yet different); I cannot know directly how long I was "out," but that "out" is indubitable. Yet, were there nothing recognized as "me" on waking, I could not say _I_ wake up. That this is difficult to explain should not blind me to the fact that I re -cognize myself; the lapse, however long, to put it paradoxically, was _my_ lapse. Yet if I was unconscious, non -recognitive, during the lapse, can I hold that my unity -continuity was existent at that time? My theory of the person seems to be in dire straits if I continue to hold that conscious unity is the essence of personal being. Some modification or revision is in order.

B.   The unconscious dimensions of the person

1. I am forbidden by my theory to "go back" and integrate my past route into my present; and I am not satisfied simply to say that whatever conditions my being aware at all--be it "God"

or my "body"--renews it as if there had been no lapse.

I propose rather to extend the scope of <u>mentality</u> to include a quality of unity-continuity that is without either self -consciousness or consciousness and yet is potentially conscious and self-conscious. In the last chapter, telescoping the essential activity-potentials in self-conscious and conscious experience in the words wanting-knowing agent, I did not emphasize the purposive (the teleological or telic) characters of these distinct but not separate activities. I am a telic agent-continuant; I interact selectively in terms of the dynamics of my interactive situation. I recognize differences of intensity and clarity within such situations. For example, there is a "burning" self-consciousness, as when I contemplate the possible cost to myself of purposely living for a set of values not socially approved. Such consciousness is different from my relatively quiescent, usual consciousness, or my sleepy consciousness, when I seem to be carried along by my sheer, telic drift.

Is it not possible to hypothesize a kind of being-becoming, neither "burning," "quiescent," nor "sleepy," that still is telic or goal-directed? Such being-becoming could not be said to be conscious in any usual sense, even though it would be capable of maintaining itself in response to its ambient. Let us take a closer look.

I have already appealed to the notion of potentiality--not logical possibility--to point to the fact that an activity can become, within limits, what it is not actually realizing in a given situation. Potentiality is not zero-being; it is not being independent of any activity; it is a dimension of that activity, "ready" to act but not actual. Why not take a further step and hold that there is a kind of telic unity, related to a person's conscious-selfconscious unity -continuity, that is ready to become conscious and self -conscious even though its telic directedness is un-conscious? Such unconscious potential-for-consciousness, and this in different degrees, is what we seem to have in sleep. Conscious beings can become unconscious, remain telic, and can return to such consciousness as their natures allow. The unconscious maintains goals-and-activities "potentially" that are not without similarity to what is known in conscious-selfconscious activity. We do, after all, reasonably ascribe unconscious telic thrust to subhuman forms of life where self-consciousness is almost certainly absent, where "consciousness" is present only in the sense that the living being is responsive in terms of its dominant telic aim.

I suggest, therefore, that "sleep" does not characterize beings who cannot become conscious (and, strictly speaking, I do not know what it means to say that beings who never have awareness of continuity can sleep). I am hypothesizing that there are levels of mentality defined by telic being-becoming. And the human level of such telic directedness is the level of telic being-becoming that is potentially conscious and self

-conscious. Sleep does not "precede" conscious awakeness; it characterizes a state of potentiality of a conscious being that is to be understood within the total context of that being's continuity.

2. I hypothesize, then, (in order to understand the phase of personal being that is continuous between being awake and deep sleep), a quality of telic, mental, unity that is not "peripherally" or "dimly" conscious but unconscious, and yet carries on activities characteristic of that person only. Hypothesizing also different degrees of telic agency, I can conclude that, say in any twenty-four hour period, I as self -conscious and conscious being--"burning" at times and "quiescent" and "sleepy" at others--have intervals during which I am "dead," in terms of self-awareness. I am not literally dead, totally non-telic, in the period of deepest sleep, because in becoming conscious and self-conscious, I can identify myself still as the unity-continuity of telic activity-potentials.

NOTE: I do not say that "burning" consciousness comes from the unconscious; I am saying that I am a mental being who does define himself in terms of different degrees of awareness. During intermittency I continue to be-become as a telic agent in my potential, unconscious-telic phase: Here I exist and change "without knowing it;" yet that change is change and not substitution. That the change is regarded as mine is the conclusion I draw from the fact that I am able, on waking, to recognize myself as the same with a difference--"I feel refreshed," "my mind is clear now."

I once listened to an Indian philosopher argue that during sleep I must be continuous as part of the One. For, he reasoned, unless some such continuity did exist, despite my unawareness, on what ground could I say, having awakened: "I slept well," or "I slept badly"? This view is not impossible, of course, but such an appeal still leaves untouched the potential latency of myself as myself (or of myself "in" the One) during this period. If there is to be latency, what forbids its being the latent potentiality of my own telic (mental) being?

Some theistic thinkers, like Augustine and Descartes, hold that there is a lapse of non-existence terminated by the re-creation of the person, consistent with his past, by God. I see nothing illogical in this view either, but I prefer not to introduce another agency or bridge (such as the brain), especially since this mediating being must itself then have different levels of awareness and degrees of latent potentiality attributed to it. I prefer rather to reason by extending what I find already in my experience, namely, different degrees or shades of vividness, intensity, and clarity. Thus, with Brand Blanshard, I would say (without restricting myself to thought alone, as he does in this passage): "We conceive the emergence of thought [the emergence of conscious goal-seeking] as a very long, slow process, whose beginnings, while the same in principle with what followed, would be unrecognizable as the same except in the light of this principle."[2] Once I can maintain the concept of unconscious telic (mental) agency, I find it more reasonable to regard particular instances of my unconscious intermittency understandable, in principle, in terms of my conscious unity-continuity.

Clearly then, I am proposing different "degrees" of telic unity and awareness as the pervasive agency in the varying phases of my mental being-becoming, as the subliminal telic phase of the self-identifying continuity of my personal existence. This subliminal phase is not to be considered as a bridge "between" conscious stages, or as an addendum to the conscious and self-conscious. The individual subliminal "activity" is a phase of a person's mental being-becoming insofar as its telic working may be understood in terms analogous to the aims the person himself knows in consciousness and self-consciousness. It is this subliminal telic agency --neither the pervasive soul, nor the brain, nor the cosmic One, nor the cosmic Creator--that, as part of the mental datum -and-continuant person, can be said to be the person during the unconscious intervals of his existence.

3. My account of intermittency thus far has been restricted to a description and interpretation of the telic unity and continuity of conscious and self-conscious I-existence. Now, in order to account for self-identity despite intermittency of

both consciousness and self-consciousness, I am extending the conception of person to include mental telic agency that can be defined as continuous with the telic dynamics consciously experienced by the person. I am at the same time suggesting that the essence of a unitary person is telic thrust that maintains itself at various levels of personal being including the unconscious, telic level.

I remember Alfred North Whitehead's remark (to a class) to the effect that "if you are to do metaphysics you must stretch your metaphysical imagination to see that what constitutes a crowbar is continuous with what constitutes a plant, a mind and a God." I am asking here that we try to conceive a mental, microscopic, telic phase of the unity-continuity we call a person. This phase is not a de-graded, or up-graded, "animal" form of being; it is a personal form of agency. The person can now be said to be capable of responding to the world--within which he lives and which, within limits, his active nature selects--at many "levels" or in many "dimensions." These dimensions and levels are activated both by inner, telic rhythms and by environmental stimuli to which he can be sensitive.

To take an illustration from normal life: the alarm clock I set to awaken me at 2:00 a.m. (three hours after falling asleep) did not do so. I may explain that I was so tired that I did not stir until about 6:00 a.m. when the noise of traffic did awaken me. I suspect that a shooting pain would have awakened me earlier. This means that during sleep my activity -potential is such that I still can be responsive to certain stimuli. When the time comes that I simply can make no differential response to any stimuli at all, I am no longer asleep but mentally dead, whether I am biologically dead or not.

Much during our conscious and self-conscious experience is explained by such mental latency. For example, I must often stop and wait for the name of a person, place, or thing to "come to me." We can account for this process of "coming to me" if we postulate ongoing telic activity of which we are not aware at the time. Such unconscious activity is usually supportive of my conscious purpose. On the other hand, the fact that ideas come to me "out of the blue," or are not always supportive of the dominant conscious trend, suggest that "work" is going on in me that is not "within my control" and yet is not alien to my conscious activities.

I am not competent to interpret the many different kinds of unconscious activity and behavior (such as somnambulism), but, before turning to "the unconscious," we might reflect further on the bare skeleton I have been setting forth as sleep -unconscious, especially my falling asleep with my own consent. When I fall asleep, I proceed by eliminating as far as possible from my attention the "outer stimuli" and the "inner objects" that normally constitute the "content" of my consciousness; "I let my mind go blank," as far as my normal waking concerns remain within my control. With such experiences of "losing myself" before us, I ask: "What kind of being would I be if I had no conscious, directive thoughts and objects?"

In answering this question I invoke the kind of telic being that I have postulated as continuant of me during sleep, a telic unity without specific objects or objectives of the sort I am aware of in my conscious-selfconscious periods. It might seem reasonable to suppose that telic mentality in fact has no objects or objectives, no activity of its own, as it were. But the plethora of data in our daily lives--such as my suddenly or gradually recollecting circumstances and names I "had completely forgotten for years"--forces me to postulate a dimension of my being that makes its "own" difference, yet is continuous with my conscious-selfconscious unity. I consciously "give it tasks" and I often am presented with an accomplishment; I seem to get an answer to a question if I lay it "aside." That is, intermittency of that question often brings me (no one else) the answer I could not consciously or purposely control. Yet the fact is that what I could not "dredge up," as the answer I wanted, is now recognized as the desired answer.

Thus, mental purposiveness may go on as a dimension of my being even though its existence has objectives and contents that are indeed often beyond my ken and my control. Once I am asleep, or once I yield my ordinary states, this unconscious dimension not only persists with its level of activity but, as our dreams dramatically suggest, achieves objectives that are not completely unrelated to the drifts of our conscious lives. Without sponsoring any one theory of dreams (and of other activities that go on without my conscious direction), it seems clear that what does go on can be related to the dynamics of my ongoing life as a person.

To summarize: there are no islands cut away from the mainland of my conscious life. To the extent that I come to make sense of what does go on in these "intervals," the products, like peninsulas, extend the conscious mainland. This conception of the person as a complex telic unity whose activities wax and wane may help us toward better understanding of what is involved in the total self-identity we experience directly in our primary conscious experience. To suppose that the unconscious telic agency we are postulating acts in ways entirely different from the ways of our varied conscious experience does not cohere with the degree of harmony that characterizes our conscious and self-conscious experience.

C. Personal unconsciousness and unusual unconscious
     activities

1. The hypothesis proposed would, as far as I can see, also be coherent with much at least of what goes on in an hypnotic trance, or in those states of unusual consciousness that supplement or cooperate with some phases of our conscious

existence. The person who has allowed himself to be hypnotized has agreed, we might say, to become responsive to an indefinite range of suggestions--yet, presumably, within the range of his constitutional activity-potentials. The person who is active in hypnosis, or who is under anesthesia, or who, by mind-controlling exercises, is able to shut away his usual sensory-perceptual-conceptual world, is able to act at a different level, and in response to an ambient not within the "normal" range of his activity-potentials. Other phases of his telic activity-potentials now are able to be sensitive to ambients that ordinarily lie outside the range of his responsiveness.

In other words, persons seem to be beings who not only act and change and grow in certain ways under "normal" environmental presses and inner demands, but are also capable of actively responding to, and reaching for, ambients usually subliminal. Such dimensions of telic sensitivity, of relatively active and relatively passive response, should not be minimized in a day when different forms of depth-therapy and the variety of parapsychic phenomena are properly receiving more attention. My peripheral consciousness, my unconscious being, and my conscious and fully self-conscious being are different currents of one telic unity that can be actively responsive to a wider range of challenge, nourishment, and threat than I normally keep in focus. But when I was a child, I dreamed as a child, had the thresholds of a child, was as suggestible as a child. Now that I am an adult, I dream as a person whose undergoings have influenced and can influence the range of my latent and potential sensitivity. I am responsive within the potentiality available to me in the context of my development and achievement thus far.

2. Accordingly, what characterizes all of our personal experience is shifting regnancy and drift within a complex unity. Hence, the picturesque aptness in Havelock Ellis' description of the "rationality" of the conscious: "Sleeping consciousness, we may even imagine as saying to itself in effect: `Here comes our master, Waking Consciousness, who attaches such mighty importance to reason and logic and so forth. Quick! gather things up, put them in order--any order will do--before he enters to take possession.'"[3] It is these gradations of regnancy that must be borne in mind when I define the person as that telic, self-identifying unity of activity-potentials best characterized in consciousness as sensing, remembering, imagining, thinking, feeling, emoting, willing, oughting, and aesthetic and religious appreciating. Our reason for defining ourselves as persons in terms of these interpenetrating activity-potentials is that they are irreducible ultimates in conscious-selfconscious mentality. Our unconscious mentality is to be understood in terms of its coherence with what is thus given in conscious personal mentality.

This line of argument is obviously congenial to the view that an amoeba, a worm, an ant, a frog, a mouse, a cat, a dog, a seal, a chimpanzee are such telic (mental) unities whose nature is to be defined by their kinds of activity-potentials. For, in the last analysis, we cannot but move by reasonable analogy from what we as persons can do to what they can do, be it better or not. It is a shallow reasoning which concludes that personal consciousness is that of a higher animal plus so much of this and plus so much of that. The assumption is too readily made that since physiologically the differences between man and animal involve additions in man, such as the frontal lobe, then the differences in personal consciousness are to be seen as similarly "additive." There is no way of escape from describing our antecedents in evolution by analogy with our dependable insights into what are our own psycho-physiological natures.

D.   Personal identity and the unconscious

In our day, personal consciousness is often regarded, rather strangely, as an addition to the unconscious, a psychic realm of being to which the conscious person is no more privy than he is to the electrical fields in his brain. The unconscious is not intermittent; it is the continuing foundation of the conscious, in a manner similar to that proposed by those who regard the body as the continuant basis of consciousness. Indeed, changes in both consciousness and in bodily behavior are often held to be the product of ferment that takes place in the unconscious. For some the unconscious is the hidden, determining source of all that occurs in the lives of persons.

The debate about the relation of the unconscious to body and to consciousness is too complex for adequate discussion here. I shall limit myself to asking what reasons warrant holding any such "independent" unconscious as my unconscious. This involves considering briefly the basis for referring to any states as mine: my past, my sleep, my dream.

1. The scope of I-my.

It is no doubt clear that we use "my" to fence off I (me) from what is not-I. The question is: What determines where the fence goes? It seems plain to me that "my" and "mine" are not simple synonyms for I. (I shall italicize I hereafter only where the context will be clearer.)

There is a first possessive sense of "my." It refers to I insofar as I can control the activities that I undergo. Hence, to the extent that I speak of anything as "completely beyond my control," then it is completely other than I or my. But to say: "I am responsible for that act, but the consequences turned out to be beyond my control," is to say that agency other-than-I took over where my agency was limited. (Other senses of "my," such as my son, my book, my university, involve, sooner or later, some degree of efficacy and preference in my relation to my agency.)

This first (possessive) sense of my is related to "my" as constitutive, that is, to "my" as defining what I am (as opposed to any other being). This constitutive I-my thus refers to the contours of the activity-potentials that constitute the scope of what I am. I have no control over the final scope of the activity-potentials that define the limits of what I can become, as opposed to what other beings are and can become. The first sense (possessive I-my) cannot exist without the constitutive sense, that is, the activity-potentials whose scope defines what I can control. This distinction between the constitutive I and the possessive I-my (mine) will help us to think more clearly about the relation of the unconscious that is presumed to be beyond the constitutive I-my in so much depth psychology.

"Entirely my own," if I am correct, accordingly refers to whatever I can be only insofar as I exist and act as I do or can. I may, of course, be wrong about my actual power in a given situation. After all, I did not create my constitutive activity-potentials. But the changes in my development, or in the world, insofar as they are due to my direction, are mine (possessive) to the degree that they are within my control.

Accordingly, then, I can refer to beings and events in the I-my range insofar as I can claim them as my consciously intended acts. For example, my fantasies are mine to a greater degree than my nightmares. The latter, unwanted as they are, are mine presumably because in my past experience I provided conditions for the occurrences. My learned dispositions, similarly, are my dispositions even if I can no longer control them or alter them, because, presumably, they were "intended" developments, acquired, largely, by I at some point in my (I -my) earlier history. They may now be "second-nature" and beyond the control of my present efforts. But they are mine because they are an acquired aspect of I-my constitutive activities. Accordingly, at any stage in I-my development, whether it be by maturation or learning, I am both my constitutive, agent-person (I-my), and my acquired dispositions (possessive I-my).

2. Difficulties in a Freudian view of the unconscious

If these senses of I-my are at all valid, can we accept views of the unconscious as the basic continuant of which the conscious I (constitutive-my) is a product? I shall limit myself to what seems basic in the view of Freud. I am not suggesting that Freud had one clearcut view of the unconscious, but what I am presenting here has become for many essential to any adequate view of the unconscious.

For Freud, the ego (I-my) is a differentiation of the primordial energy of the unconscious. The constitutive pleasure-seeking, non-moral, non-rational, non-social energies of the unconscious were "in the beginning" unable to derive a maximum of pleasure in a partly hostile, social, and natural environment. To cope with unwanted conflicts the unconscious delegated some of its energy to essentially perceptual -conceptual functions, which make up the conscious ego. In the total economy of the human being, therefore, the aim of the ego is to be aware of both the demands of the pleasure-seeking unconscious and of the environment, with a view to maximizing pleasure and minimizing needless conflict.

I doubt that this transaction can bear close scrutiny, for one wonders how a completely non-rational process, the unconscious, would become so aware of its predicament as to delegate some of its energy for the purpose so contrary to its own nature.[4]

Since I am concerned here with theoretical consequences of conceptualizing the unconscious as having its own generative powers from which the constitutive I-my is formed, I shall continue to focus on the concept typified by Freud's use. And, indeed, an anomalous situation faces us. For we are given to understand that the initially important ego, unable to produce changes in the pleasure-seeking demands of the unconscious id, does acquire enough perceptive and reasoning power to affect the expression of these unconscious urges. Indeed, in Freud's thought the ego plays a part in developing the super-ego, the acquired moral monitor, and thus extends its censorship over such unconscious pleasure-seeking as would eventuate in serious conflict with the social environment. (The super-ego is sometimes pictured as originating, in part at least, in the unconscious.) However, even if the super-ego's origin is sometimes ambiguous in Freud, there is no doubt that it becomes the automatic inhibitor, or internalized monitor, grounded in the edicts of this ego as it becomes aware of what would be unproductive conflicts between the pleasure-urges and social demands.

What is fascinating about this evolutionary, prudential relation between the unconscious and the super-ego is that, once the ego appears, it seems impossible to keep it powerless. It is no mere cavil to express surprise that in the non -rational, non-social, passionately wayward womb of the id there should be born, without benefit of rational father even, an ego that governs itself by rational principles and even develops its own autonomous unity. "Thus in its relation to the Id it [ego] is like a man on horseback, who has to hold in check the superior strength of the horse; with this difference that the rider seeks to do so with his own strength while the Ego uses borrowed forces."[5] Indeed, why have it, if it is all but powerless? Still, the ego, once it appears (having "borrowed forces" whence?), clearly has an effect on the unconscious and its ways--which it presumably could not even know! If, indeed, the I (as the ego) has its origin in the unconscious, (or, in my terms, if the unconscious is I-my), there are serious consequences for Freudian therapy. For to hold that success in therapy depends on the ego being where the unconscious is, this requires that the unconscious be re -conceived and be I-my in both constitutive and possessive senses.

In short, if the unconscious, no longer the primordial source of the ego, is rather a dimension of I-my (constitutive and possessive), then the relations of the unconscious and the conscious are at least no longer opaque. We must not forget that, even on a Freudian view, the urges ascribed to the unconscious do in the last analysis resemble those of which we are conscious, and the "cunning" of the unconscious has its exemplars in conscious experience. For example, was it not Freud's observations of the resistance consciously experienced by his patients as they tried to tell their therapist about their conscious disturbances that led Freud to postulate unconscious activity? The symptoms which could not be accounted for by reference to physiological processes Freud explained by hypothesizing psychic, telic, unconscious "powers" at odds with those found in consciousness. Yet these powers, presumably beyond the control of the ego (not in the sphere of possessive I-my) can, on Freud's view, be understood only by analogy with processes and goals that persons know in consciousness (hence are not discontinuous with the constitutive I-my?).

In sum, the unconscious is not, somehow, the enduring unity -continuity upon which the ego (constitutive I-my) depends. Rather must the unconscious be understood as within the scope of constitutive I-my activity-potentials; and since it can to some degree affect and be affected by them, the telic, mental unconscious is also in different degrees within the sphere of possessive I-my.

E. A personalistic overview of the unconscious and
unconscious processes

1. It is time to draw together different strands in the
conception of the person, with special reference to the
relation of conscious-selfconscious and unconscious dimensions.
My basic suggestion is that unconscious processes could not be
called I-mine if they were not in fact similar to those in my
conscious experience. On the most striking, opposing view, the
Freudian unconscious has its ego, since the ego is the
differentation (or some sort of derivative) of the unconscious.
Yet the therapeutic approach to the unconscious is through the
conscious ego, so the ego presumably, in some way, affects the
unconscious and is not simply its slave. Freud's theory is not
coherent with such agency. Moreover, if the ego influences
unconscious activities, those activities can hardly be so alien
to those in consciousness. The unconscious is too blind to
"produce" the kind of ego that will be a guide to reality.
The ego, in turn, is too subservient to have influence on its
unconscious.

Since, in fact, mutual influence of the unconscious and the
ego is so significant, I am proposing an inclusive telic unity
(constitutive I-my) in which unconscious work is not
intrinsically alien to the conscious activities. Accordingly,
the telic unconscious processes beyond my normal awareness and
control are not the source of my ego (I). These unconscious

processes are at least remotely analogous to those that constitute my conscious and self-conscious being and can be influenced by my (possessive) conscious life in some degree even as they in turn influence conscious activities.

However, to include unconscious telic activities in the dynamics of the telic person (constitutive I-my)[6] is not to support an unconscious system of "forces" that governs conscious activities (ego) derived to serve them. These unconscious processes (be they Freudian and Jungian, or...), may indeed constitute dimensions of personal being not open to inspection, but there are no strong grounds for granting them complete autonomy, let alone allowing them to become the condition of the constitutive and possessive I-my.

2. We may now put the resultant view in the context of our larger thesis concerning the person. The unconscious, once we stop thinking of "it" as an island unconnected with the mainland of the self-identifying person, may be said to function in ways related to the person's total mental continuity and unity. The I that we are certain of is the unity of the conscious-selfconscious datum person. Evidence in the datum person warrants the inference that this I is not confined to telic, conscious and self-conscious mentality. Much of the datum person's experience is illuminated by postulating (constitutive I-my) unconscious telic activities. As in the case of sleep, we can reasonably grant unconscious telic agency and "cognition," but neither as powers

discontinuous completely with such processes as we find in consciousness, nor as forces that cannot be influenced by constitutive I-my activities. Actually, much of the unconscious dimensions of personal action can be understood largely in terms of the possessive I-my that is (or at some time has been) within the scope of the conscious-selfconscious person.

The unconscious, accordingly, is to be considered a contemporaneous aspect of my personal being (constitutive I -my). I-my does not always operate within privately or socially approved aims. Still, would any depth therapy be possible if we presupposed that the work of the unconscious was initially other than, and could never be influenced by, the conscious and self-conscious telic activity-potentials of the person?

3. What Freudian and other depth psychologies do for us is to broaden our conception of the dimensions of mental being that constitute a person. The more specific dynamics of those dimensions, whether they be the instinctual urges of Freud, or the Jungian collective unconsciousness, will need to be justified on the basis of the evidence. My contention here is that these "depth" dimensions of personal being do operate in relation to the conscious wanting-knowing person, and they do carry on functions, with a relative degree of autonomy, which, as therapy shows, meet some demands of the person as we know him. Thus, whether the person sleeps and therein carries on a

subsidiary life that both reflects and alters his conscious action and purpose; or whether the person carries on unconscious activities that, as creative invention often indicates, supplement what is experienced in conscious telic activity, the person is at work in different ways as a mental being with complex ends. While I do not know by inspection what is going on in my unconscious, the inferences that are reasonably possible from what is present in consciousness justify my believing that what does go on there is presumably related to, and not in essence different from, what I can be aware of.

4. Again, while it is beyond my competence to pass judgment on, or reinterpret with confidence phenomena that need expert analysis--such as somnambulism, trances, amnesia, hypnosis, split personality, and other psychic phenomena--it seems clear that they give evidence of different degrees of unconscious activity and responsiveness to problems in the total person. I urge only that, instead of being partitioned _off_ from _I_-activities, they be partitioned _into_ _the_ _total_ _responsivity_ _and_ _telic_ _unity_ _of_ _the_ _person_. The person may well be solving some problem in his being, or exercising a capacity, whether in a trance or in hypnosis, that is unusual. The theoretical obligation remains, whether we deal with such capacities, or others that seem to be extra-sensory, telepathic, or clairvoyant, to evaluate the evidence for them and examine their links with the complex, conscious and self-conscious

unity of the person.

We have created unnecessary problems by being all too ready to restrict the boundaries of personal being, or to compound it out of the parts, or to express what is unusual in exaggerated terms that suggest a greater difference in activity than is reasonable, given the evidence. For example, to speak of "total amnesia" may make sense in a defined psychological context, that is, when a segment of forgotten material is so large that a portion of a person's life is beyond his recognition or recall, with the result that he does not know who he is. Thus, by the "total amnesia" of a person, we mean, for example, that he has forgotten his name, where he came from, his family, and the usual factors by which he identifies himself and orients his life, such as his trade. Thus to talk of this person's having "total" amnesia is to invite problems. For the individual still has an enormous range of conscious activities and memories available to him. Total amnesia, literally interpreted, would take him back to his conception in the womb. After all, he is still speaking a language, walking, eating, taking streetcars, and so on.

5. The phenomena to which we assign different "degrees" of unconsciousness have thus led me to enlarge the concept of the self-identifying person to include unconscious processes that are intelligible only as phases of a more comprehensive telic unity. The processes that we call subconscious and unconscious

"incubation" seem to be ways in which some of the ranging work of the person goes on. If anything, all peripheral and unconscious processes justify our characterizing personal unity in telic terms--not as a mathematical identity, not merely as a combination of functions, but as a continuing thrust toward completion or reorganization of what is retained. In this context, F. R. Tennant's basic thesis takes on even more meaning: "Consciousness is not given in atoms; its smallest portion is a process, and the simplest portion is complex.... The mind must be provisionally and analogically conceived as having structure, as a system of systems elaborated by [I should prefer "united in"] one and the same subject [person]."[7]

Though hinting at the problem now and then, I seem, rather oddly, to have devoted much space to the unity of the person without discussing the relation of mind to body. Perhaps there has been a method in my madness--if only to have indicated that one can speak of the person and his unconscius activities without reference to any special view of the body. This fact, in turn, suggests that we can know some of a person's experience, as he undergoes it and identifies himself in it, that has no necessary reference to his body. Our task now is to continue to develop an adequate theory of the person by conceiving the nature of the person's relation to his physiological organism.

Notes for Chapter Two

1. I find persuasive H. D. Lewis's critique of S. Shoemaker's discussion of the criteria of self-identity in _Self-Knowledge_ and _Self-Identity_, 1963. But while Lewis' own view of the awareness of self-identity is more plausible than Shoemaker's (see _The Elusive Mind_, 1969, 221-226, and especially 240f.), I am doubtful that Lewis could sustain his claim that I am immediately aware of my identity in directly successive moments and over intermittency if there were no experience of "me -again" (to which I have appealed as the basis of my affirmation of self-identity).

2. Brand Blanshard, _Nature of Thought_, vol. 1 (London: Allen and Unwin, 1939), 513.

3. I owe this quotation to James G. Miller, _Unconsciousness_ (New York: Wiley and Sons, 1942), 283, who quotes Ellis, _The World of Dreams_ (Boston: Houghton Mifflin, 1911), 10.

4. For an illuminating, brief outline of the psycho-logic of the unconscious in Freud and others, including Jung, see Orville S. Walters, "Theology and Changing Concepts of the Unconscious" in _Religion and Life_ (Spring 1968). Aware of the shifts in Freud's own thinking, Walters has support from other scholars when he contends that while

Freud began with a (legitimate) hypothetical construct of the unconscious, he (and many of his followers) talked of this unconscious and its dynamics as if these were the result of observations upon which other theories were properly based. Walters is also cognizant of the fact that the ego lost its servility and developed more autonomy in the ego-psychology that later developed in part from Freudian and from Jungian beginnings. Freud himself at one point said: "This ego developed out of the id, it forms with it a single biological unit, it is only a specially modified peripheral portion of it, and it is subject to the influences and obeys the suggestions that arise from the id." I owe this quotation (italics added) to Walters, ibid., 6, quoting from Freud's Works, vol. 19 (London: Hogarth Press, 1963), 133.

5. Sigmund Freud, The Ego and the Id, (New York: International Universities Press, 1957), 29-30.

6. This view differs from that of my teacher, Edgar S. Brightman, who tended to regard unconscious process beyond the control of "normal" consciousness as "intimate partner of our reflective conscious selves, but no more a part of them than are other reflective selves or sub-personal selves." E. S. Brightman, Person and Reality, ed. Peter A. Bertocci, et al (New York: Ronald Press, 1958), 174; and see 207-209. See also

"Brightman's View of the Self, the Person, and the
Body," 8 (<u>Philosophical</u> <u>Forum</u>, 1950): 21-28.

7.   Frederick R. Tennant, <u>Philosophical</u> <u>Theology</u>, vol. 1
(Cambridge University Press, 1928), 42, 120.

CHAPTER THREE

The Person's Body

A.   Present status of the argument

Our reasoning thus far has applied the basic thesis that any interpretation of ourselves and of other beings should not neglect, distort, or render unintelligible what is undergone in conscious and self-conscious experience. As C. I. Lewis has said: "That which explains experience is always something which the experience in question gives us some reason (some partial ground) for assuming."[1] The method of beginning with the data in conscious experience does not entail the conclusion that the person is no more than his conscious experience. For example, in chapter 2 we inferred, from what is given in conscious experience, that a person's unconscious processes are more understandable as "extensions" of the dynamics of the self-identifying person. Our task now is to see what we can reasonably say about the person in the light of his conscious experience of his body.

1. I approach this task by expanding aspects of what has already been said about the datum person. In essentially Cartesian fashion,[2] I have urged that nothing is more certain, psychologically and logically, than that I am, as a datum person, a complex unity of distinguishable but interrelated activities and their potentials:[3] sens_ing_, remember_ing_, think_ing_, feel_ing_, emot_ing_, will_ing_, ought_ing_, and aesthetic and religious appreciat_ing_. What consciousness and mentality would mean other than some form of these telic activity-potentials I know not. But we never undergo these without _their_ "objects" or "objectives." In other words, once personal consciousness appears, there it is with its own experienc_ing_, and at any _moment_, the "objects" or "objectives" of its experiencing. (While I shall continue to use the words "experience," "experiencing," and "experienc_ed_" as if they were confined to the conscious dimension of the person, it should be remembered that these words, already weighted in favor of knowing, include unconscious, telic dimensions of personal mentality.)

2. Granted the unity-continuity of these activity -potentials, even as their "objects" and "objectives" change, our task is to discover the relationships that exist within experience and "whatever is" beyond experience--for example, a Berkeleyan God, a system of non-mental processes, or a society of psychic beings that compose my body and the

world. In particular, what is the relation of the level of mentality (that I have so far described as the person in his conscious, self-conscious, and inferred unconscious activity-potentials) to what I shall call "the person's body?"

B.   The act of cognitive reference and the mind-body relation

1. It seems to me that once we fully appreciate the difference between a cognitive and any other process, it becomes unreasonable to hold that a person, in his cognitive activities at least, can be identified with any processes as defined by the physiologist. I am aware of various attempts to soften the stark contention that all mental events are physiological events, but I find them ultimately half-way houses open only to those who do not see adequately the difference between cognitive activities and cortical events. What is the difference I have in mind--one that, by itself, is basic to my differentiation between mental and non-mental?

Any experience as experience (anger, blue shape, "and") is neither correct nor incorrect. Yet when I experience cognitively, I am still experiencing. However, mark the difference! I am now referring whatever I am experiencing beyond the experience itself, and claiming to know what I am referring to. Knowing, then, is the kind of experiencing that, whatever else, consists in referring beyond itself; cognition of any sort, correct or incorrect, could not take place without this experiencing of objective reference. Moreover, this (cognitive) referring is distinct from any other experiencing, or event, because it can be mistaken in its cognitive claims. In particular, what can it possibly mean to say that a cell or an electrical field "refers" or, in referring, is correct or incorrect? Again, what would it mean to say that the mental occurrence, such as "I experience cold," is, as experience, correct or incorrect? Even if I affirm that my experience of cold is "of the room" I am in, I refer the experienced object beyond itself as an experience; and if its claim is to know that the room is not cold, the fact still remains that I experienced "cold." The reference was incorrect; the experiencing cannot be incorrect.

This stark difference between cognitive, objective reference and any other kind of experience or event is fundamental to my claim that I am the kind of being that can go on experiencing an object-experienced even when the referring of that object beyond itself turns out to be incorrect. It is this fact, that I can claim truth or falsity for any referred experience, that leads me to the clearest instance of the distinction between mental and non-mental being. Were there no telic activity of this sort, I might be willing to say that mental activities are understandable as brain-events. [4]

2. Let us take a closer look at my query: Does it make any sense to say that a physiological occurrence is in error? What goes on in any brain cell or system of brain cells, as described by the biologist or bio-chemist, are changes none of which refers change beyond itself. If we conceive of these changes as being ultimately electrical, we are equally lost. For what can it possibly mean to say that a spatiotemporal electrical system refers beyond itself? Yet if we follow those who would _identify_ mind and brain and hold that the brain knows, we are forced to claim that changes, physiological or electrical, can know--a meaningless claim because these changes _as changes_ involve neither objective reference, nor truth, nor error. There simply is no way of "translating" error into some set of brain-events. [5] Only some form of picture-thinking (such as "in" the brain), can seduce us into identifying mental activities with brain-activities. [6]

Speaking of picture-thinking, it should be noted that, however difficult it may be to picture mental activities without brain activities, it is certainly no easier to picture what it can mean to say that mind-activities are brain-events. I am not, for reasons soon to be advanced, about to say, with Descartes, that _all_ mental activities are non-spatial. But we miss the basic point of Descartes'

insight if we do not focus on the difference between brain
-cells and brain-events that are "spread out" in a skull,
and experiences that are not spatially extended. Non
-Cartesians must make clear what it can possibly mean to say
that there is "extension" of any sort in our experiencing of
consistency and contradiction, of willing, of oughting, of
appreciating, and of desiring. What, for example, can it
mean to talk about logical relations of consistency or
contradiction as spatiotemporal motions of cell-electricity?
When I say that events "follow" each other in my brain I
certainly do not mean the kind of logical "follow" I
experience when I say: If A is greater than B, and B is
greater than C, it follows that A is greater than C.

In any case, while I would agree that the difference
between extended and non-extended being is a basis for
distinguishing between mental and non-mental, I find the
capacity for cognitive reference even more telling. For I
cannot understand what it would mean to say that true and
false are some changes in or among cells, as defined by
biologists, or in or among some physical motions, as
described by physicists.

3. To these considerations I add what I find implicit in the
whole notion of a person as a self-identifying, cognitive
agent. That is, without the unity-continuity of a knower,
there can be no understanding of meaning, which always
involves reference beyond the experienced state. Since the

whole theory of the person ultimately turns on this fact that a person is a unified agent who cannot, especially as cognitive, be understood in physicalistic or physiological terms, I shall develop the thesis I have just advanced.

First, knowing is being, to be sure, but it is a kind of being that is different from any other kind of being (or event). Now, whatever else I am or do, I claim to know. Thus I make cognitive proposals like: "That book is black." In so doing, I am proposing-agent. That is, I claim that my experiencing of book and black refers to something not my experiencing and not my referring. To claim to know always involves referring in this way, be the reference to my own past, to my own ongoing state, to an anticipated future, or to something other than myself. To know, accordingly, involves an irreducibly unique type of being--one that can refer.

Second, I would not have occasion to distinguish objective reference if I were always correct. At any given cognitive moment, I am psychologically certain that what is "there" is as experienced. I grant that we are all "inexpugnable realists," to use Arthur Lovejoy's term,[7] who find ourselves assuming that what we experience is as we experience it. However, whatever our final theory of knowledge, none of us can deny that we are often in error. The existence of error means that any knower must distinguish between the object as experienced and the object he claims to know.

Third, a theory of mind and body must make room for this cognitive situation. When I perceive the coiled rope as a snake, and then discover that I perceive "snake" that cannot be said to be "rope," where shall I locate the "snake?" That is, where shall I locate my error? Can I locate it in the rope? No. Can I locate it in some brain event? Surely not. For, whether I perceive "rope" or "snake," the same (sensory) physiological or electrical events take place in the optic nerve, thalamus, and occipital areas of the brain. When I later discover that what I perceive is a rope and not a snake, can I say that the snake-reference was an erroneous brain-event? Hardly. My experienced "snake" is no less an experience, although I now know that my initial referential perception was erroneous. In short, neither the "locus" of error, nor the objective reference of my snake-experience, can be assimilated to, or identified with, any event in my brain or in the rope.

Fourth--and I draw my basic conclusion--if I say that all events are spatiotemporal in the physicalistic sense, I place myself in a hopeless quandary. No such event can be itself and refer beyond itself; no such event can be correct or incorrect; yet "true" and "false" are integral to any cognitive situation. Accordingly, even if I had no other reason for believing in distinctive and irreducible mental agency, I would contend: Something there must be which undergoes an experience, refers it to something beyond the experience itself, and still is the "locus" for the erroneous assertion. For the assertion--"That is a snake" --existed "somehow" and "somewhere" as a proposal, and I simply cannot say that this erroneous asserting could be "in the rope." And since I simply cannot conceive what it would mean to "locate" error "among" or "in," or as "somehow," brain-events, I conclude that the wanting-knowing agent must exist if I am to make any reasonable sense out of the existence of true and false claims. The proposing agent may well be related to other events, but he never is the non-cognitive events or changes referred to.

C.   The primary _I_ and _my_

From now on, then, I shall assume that I cannot strictly identify myself, _I_, (the wanting-knowing agent at least), with bio-chemical or physiological events. I am not more certain of the existence of my body than I am of myself as a proposing agent. I still need to understand, however, what the relation of _I_ is to what I call "my body." I have already undertaken to explain what I mean when I speak of my unconscious (mental) dimension. I shall now try to define _my_ and _I_ in the primary sense and explore the meaning and relation of _my_ body to _I_.

1. In the primary _I_ is included all that I have already advanced in chapter 2 as the constitutive-_I_, the self-identifying, complex unity of certain distinct but interpenetrating activity-potentials. These activity-potentials, I re-emphasize, do not exist in abstraction from their objects and objectives, even though they outlive any specific objects and objectives. Thus I do not sense without sens_ing_ some _sensory qualia_. Specific objects and objectives, therefore, come and go, but the unity of activities (and their potentials for further experience) are the primary _I-my_. (I shall not italicize _I-my_ hereafter unless context requires.)

2. I now advance proposals that require further explication. The primary I-my is defined (a) by the nature and scope of the unified activity-potentials, (b) by whatever objects and objectives that may be found to constitute its very being in contradistinction from any other being. Insofar as this primary I-my is found to include unlearned objects and objectives, it is distinct from its acquired and learned objects and objectives. But these learned objects and objectives may become so much "second nature" that they are I-mine in the secondary (possessive) sense, especially as opposed to factors in the world that are in no way dependent upon I-my and I-mine for their existence and changes.

Let me expand on what I mean. If my thinking-activities are found to involve unlearned norms of consistency, or if my emotive-activities are found to include, for example, unlearned fear-and-its-object-objective, these are aspects of primary I-my. The _particular_ _ways_ _of_ _thinking_ that I learn, along with the specific fears that I acquire, are, accordingly, I-mine in a secondary sense. In this possessive sense, "I-mine" refers to what would not exist independently of primary I-my activity-potentials. We have already argued that my unconscious is _mine_ in the primary sense insofar as its very existence and potential are connected with I-my, but it is _mine_ in the secondary sense insofar as the specific "content" reflects modifications by I-my learning.

The same line of reasoning leads to my conclusion here: The _total_ _person_ at any point in his history involves both the primary, constitutive I-my and the secondary, possessive, I-mine whose nature will always presuppose I-my and reflect my engagements with environment(s). Indeed, I -my as a total person involves me in developing my personality (possessive I-mine), that is, all that primary I-my acquires as a result of interaction with environment(s). It is never easy to demarcate these boundaries with great confidence, and in large part because primary _I_ (I-my) cannot be-become apart from modifications resulting from interaction with particular environments. It is in this context that we may explore the meaning of I-my and my body.

D.   The person and his lived body

1. To begin with, let us note the telling contrast between my body as sensed and perceived and my logical activities. I discover that insofar as I think as opposed to merely have associations of ideas, I must connect one thought with another according to unlearned logical principles. I do not create the principles of consistency; they are given and I am subject to their formal constraints as I think. In short, I can, within limits, will to think or not to think, but once I do think, I am subject to logical norms, not of my own making, that have authority over me even when they are not obeyed.

2. I am stressing those logical norms as _given_ _within_ the constitution of I-my activity-potentials because there is another range of non-normative _givens_ in my experience that are recalcitrant factors in any attempt I make to define my body and my world. I am referring, of course, to the complex matrix of my sensory experiencing. As a sensing person I experience a range of qualities (_qualia_) that are _given_ _to_, or _taken_ _away_ _from_, my primary sensing activity. These _qualia_ _as_ _given_ are not _modes_ of, or _identical_ _with_, my sensing-capacity, for my sensing activity will be capable of other qualia after any set is gone. The colors of the cloudy sky, say, will give way as I go on sensing those of a

threatening one. But, _given_ now means given _to_ rather than given _in_, or intrinsic to I-my as sensing. Thus, specific colors, sounds, smells, and so on, do not constitute I-my in the primary sense, even though I could not define my scope as an experient without reference to some qualia.

Hence, oversimplifying, I soon learn that a vast variety of sensory qualia, with their own refractory nature and order, constitute the scope and limits of my sensory experiencing. This varied range of qualia I do not consider mine in the primary sense because, even though they hold me to their quality and order as I try to make more connections between them and between them and me, I can move from one complex sensory "world" to another; I am not confined to any one "world" as sensed.

3. Almost! For I find upon further analysis that I must make a distinction within this matrix of qualia that is before me as "the world as sensed." Within this world there is a persistent, nuclear family of qualia that is "always with me," as it were. I call these nuclear-qualia my _lived-body_. I suggest that, despite the fact that from moment to moment, from day to day, from year to year, we cannot draw a neat line separating "members" of this nuclear family from other sensory qualia, we all come to discern and identify such a complex family of qualia as "ours." Indeed, the quality and pattern of this nuclear family is sufficiently constant, for most practical purposes of daily life (and

especially in pre-reflective and non-reflective phases of our lives), that we think of I as what happens "in" and "to" this sensory nuclear family. Since it is much easier to distinguish myself in terms of "my bodily self," for the rough and ready purposes of everyday interaction, we come to identify our bodily selves with primary I-my.

All the more, then, what needs stressing here is that while each of us experiences indubitably the varied qualitative range of sensory data, none of these come initially with tags marked "my body," "the chair out there," "the twinkling star." Even the classification "sensory," as opposed to "non-sensory," is a product of reflective learning. Much discrimination precedes my gradual realization that, among the areas of refractory sensory qualia and their refractory order, there is a relatively persistent family I refer to as "my" body. To "discover" this nuclear family is to discover that I am now both "enslaved" and "empowered" (within limits) by my body.

To emphasize: I must accept the presence, quality, and order of these nuclear qualia in contrast to that of other groups and orders which, though also refractory, are not at all within my control. For example, I can move my arm, even though I cannot change the qualia I know as my arm. I cannot, to be sure, control the pattern and quality of "my pencil," but the qualia involved in "movement of my arm" are alterable in a way, and controlled in a degree that is consistently different from those "supplied" by the pencil I am moving.

At least three facts become clear. First, since I can do so little about this nucleus of sensory qualia that is "always with me," and since I come to regard this nucleus as the relatively constant _lived_ background for other ranges of sensory data, I identify _my_ body with this lived-family of sensory qualia. Second, this identification is reinforced by my ability to control, within limits, what _my_ body does or any part of _my_ body (my arm) does. Third, I can exercise no direct control over what is no part of my nuclear, lived-body.

4. A further far-reaching observation is now in order. I am never without a family of qualia that I consider mine (in large part because it is relatively constant). Indeed, my lived-body is in my "control" in ways that allow me to distinguish myself from all the other sensory regions that are not mine, and that I come to regard as the "external" world (not-_I_). When I examine the nature of this nuclear lived-body, I realize that some of the qualia in this family are extended and some are not. My auditory, olfactory, and gustatory qualia, for example, are not _as_ _such_, extended, while the visual, in particular, are. Thus my lived-body is extended in some respects only.[8] I cannot continue to hold, therefore, that primary I-my is necessarily non-extended (as I could if all of my experience was thinking in terms of

consistency). Nor can I say that mentality is <u>necessarily</u> non-extended, and especially insofar as my lived-body is involved. This does <u>not</u> mean that I-my, inclusive of my lived body, is identifiable with the events in the brain as generally conceived by physicists, chemists, and physiologists. However, since an adequate solution of the mind-body problem calls for a theory of space and time, I restrict myself to relating the person to his lived-body and Body, and to merely suggesting larger issues more pertinent here.

E.   The person, the lived-body, and the Body

When I capitalize the first letter in Body and in World or Environment, I am referring to the inferred perceptual -conceptual Order as distinct from the experienced world (environment). My immediate aim is to indicate why the distinction between the lived-body and Body (environment and Environment) arises.

1. I have argued that I come to distinguish my lived-body from my multifarious, refractory, sensory world in which I distinguish "my" pencil and "my" room from the tree yonder and the plane overhead. In distinguishing these from each other, my discrimination is guided mainly by the degree of causal control I can exert over each. I no doubt am related to, and interact with, what is not mine at all. So far as I

can tell, to the degree that I cannot control or even influence beings and events, they to that degree are not mine.[9] For our purposes here I stress the fact that, while I-my is not identical with my nuclear lived-body, my lived -body "stays with me" and remains my experiential background for the distinctions I make between my "embodied" person and the perceived-conceived Bodies of other beings (animals and persons) and of other existents.

But we must not fail to note that our lived-bodies also do not obey our every wish. We each discover that our lived-bodies respond "in their own way" to our wanting and willing. Each of us, for example, can describe the kind of qualities and relations within our lived-bodies to our physician. Our physician, however, listens to our reports and interprets what he hears and observes in the light of his constructed, scientific framework. He makes suggestions to us based upon what we report as our experience, upon what he interprets us to mean, upon what his perceptual -conceptual experience of Bodies is, and upon what he conceives to be the events in the conceptually constructed World that his learning leads him to believe are related to human lived-bodies. Briefly put, both the patient and the doctor believe that what is being experienced as normal and non-normal involves reference both to the order of lived -qualities and to the inferred Order that is not lived but believed-to-be-existent and related to each lived-body in certain orderly ways.

Accordingly, I infer both that my lived-body constitutes a varying, yet recognizable, continuing segment of my total being, but that its constraining organization requires me to explore its relation to my Body and to Environment. In short, we seek to understand what occurs in our lived-bodies by relating them to non-sensed and non-sensory aspects of I -my experience (including the unconscious), and to our Bodies and other Environmental situations that are as such no part of our lived-bodies. It would seem that what each of us experiences as his lived-body is a continuant matrix of sensory qualia that coexists with primary I-my, even though it does not exhaust I-my. As already noted, the far -from-neat definition of my lived-body goes on apace as I learn to distinguish this nuclear family of qualia from the larger "world" of sensory qualia that I designate as belonging to other than I-my and to other than my lived-body.

2. Is this lived-body mine in the same sense as the activity-potentials that constitute I-my? The answer, already partly suggested, is really yes and no. Why? I-my, in the primary sense, is defined by the activity-potentials that constitute the complex, self-identifying unity of my being. In no sense do I control the essence of the activity-potentials and the ultimate range of their

potential. Hence, I say: I am they, and what they can be; they are I-my in the sense that for me to be and become is to change and act within the never-finally-defined limits of their potential. But while I never can tell exactly how far my activity-potentials can reach, I can approach some definition of what they involve. For example, I may think about extended qualia and extended being, but my thinking -activity and its norms are non-extended.

Can I say that the family of qualia, extended and non -extended, that is my lived-body, is mine in the same way as my activity-potentials are? I can answer _yes_ insofar as a lived-body is co-existent with I-my in an inescapable way. That is, I am confined, in those qualitative areas of my experience, to the order and connections they impose upon me as I discover them. Indeed, my thinking cannot change the connections among these bodily qualia any more than it can change the order of sensory qualia of "external objects" like stones and stars. I can also answer _yes_ insofar as, having become aware of these connections, I can influence my lived-body as I conduct, within limits, my interactions with conceived situations that remain beyond my control and that I therefore call "the World beyond me".

In sum, the quality and pattern of qualia "in" my lived body differ from the rest of my sensory experience, even though they too impose on me their own order of qualiative complexity. Nevertheless, my lived-body goes "with me" as my "clothing," the bodies of other people, and specific "physical environments," like my house, do not. Within this lived-body, furthermore, I come to differentiate areas ("my arm," for example) in accordance with their significance for I-my. But these areas, in turn, have the significance for me that they do because I am constrained to observe the order that seems to govern them. Accordingly, I am less vitally affected, for example, when I file or cut my finger nails, than I am by changes in the auditory, kinesthetic, and other "more vital" qualiative families within my bodily matrix. Such changes in my lived-body indicate that the differences that I can make in my lived-body are not completely within the control of my desires and will.

3. Implicit in what has been said are the grounds for my also answering: No, my lived-body is not mine in the same primary way, for example, as logical activity is. While my lived-body would not exist independently of the activities that constitute the primary I-my, my lived-body is indeed a co-existent factor in much primary I-my experience. Nevertheless, specific qualia and the varying order within my lived-body also depend, to an extent to be discovered, upon factors beyond my control. The lived-body I had when I was five years old, twenty-five, and fifty was indeed mine, for I could identify much of I-mine in terms of each relatively constant family of qualia. However, the similarity among these families did not depend upon I-my

activities alone. Each family was _my_ _body_ and yet each gave way, despite any effort of mine, to a succeeding family. In this sense my lived-body cannot be defined exclusively as primarily I-my. Why? Because my lived-body cannot be what it is without I-my activities, and without some source other than I-my.

At this point, it would be easy to assume or infer that the "source" other than I-my is the matrix of organic situations as described by the physiologist. While I shall not try to develop the thesis here, I should argue that any such conclusion must not override what our examination has revealed, namely, that I-my non-sensory activities and lived-body are hardly copies or duplicates of organic situations. What also seems clear is: whatever is the source of I-my, I need to keep inferring situations beyond I-my in order to make reasonable sense of much that occurs in my lived-body.

What needs special stress is, nevertheless, the fact that the qualiative order that I come to realize as "my body" comes not with the label "my body"; it is a complex qualiative system that "shares" my mental life with me, in relation to other activities and dimensions of my being. Moreover, this lived-body-constellation is dependent both on I-my-existence and on "my" Body and the World impinging upon me (in ways that require further investigation). I cannot minimize the fact that, if I am to nourish my lived-body, I must do it by observing _its_ qualiative order _in_ _relation_ _to_ _whatever_ the correlations are of this body both to Unconscious Processes within me, to Processes that go on in my Body as described by the physiologist, and to the World in which the Body exists as reliably conceived by other investigators.

4. To draw minimal conclusions for a theory of the person and his body: the lived-body cannot be viewed as an "incarnation" of a mind, or as the "reflection" of physiological processes. My lived-body is primary _I-my_ in one dimension of my total continuing unity. It has independence insofar as its qualiative patterns are imposed on I-my, in whose concrete history they participate and to which they contribute. But I must also conclude that the primary I-my is neither a ghost, nor a shadow of some other being, nor a non-sensory unity bereft of qualia, nor a copy of my lived-body. I am a continuant-unity-of-activity -potentials-correlated-with-my-qualiative-family that helps me to identify myself in relation to other beings and events. More formally: A person is not a mind "in" a Body; he is a self-identifying temporal unity-continuity whose qualiative lived-body mediates what is the Body and the Environment with which he interacts.

Consequently, as we face the question as to what the nature of the inferred Body and its World is, we must not first assume the truth of a materialistic, a naturalistic, an idealistic, a pan-psychistic, a Thomistic realist, or any other world-view, <u>and</u> <u>then</u> interpret ourselves as we experience ourselves by what seems to be the consequences of the assumed views. What seems clear and central is that we are persons whose self-identifying unity includes sensory and non-sensory activities and their objects-objectives, along with a qualiative body that cannot be adequately explained without reference to a Body and Environment. What this is, and what their specific relation is to the person and his lived-body (and unconscious) is open to the most coherent interpretation of the available evidence.

F.   The person's body as a scientific construct

1. A reader might well comment: You have argued against any view of the total person that separates, as did Descartes, mind from extension. At the same time, you refused to identify the person entirely with his lived-body within the mental realm, and intimated that what is experienced therein is dependent also on its relation to some Order beyond itself.[10] At the same time, you have inveighed against views of mind and body that, without first examining the uniqueness of the cognitive situation and the uniqueness of each lived-body, tend to deduce the mind-body relation from conceptual constructs that do not take into account a person's experience of himself.

The reader is correct: an adequate treatment of the relation of the person to the Order(s) beyond himself entails a systematic epistemology and metaphysics. I here propose a first step toward a more complete philosophical understanding that is compatible with much at the scientific level of description and explanation.

2. If the drift of the considerations here proposed is correct, I must continue to reject any view of the person as identical with organic or physico-chemical events in the Body.[11] Nor do I know what to make of a strict parallelistic view according to which every psychic event has a parallel counterpart in the brain, for I do not know how this relation, if indeed parallel, could ever be ascertained. On the other hand, if I-my is an epiphenomenon of the Body, I must conclude, contrary to my experience and reason, that neither my cognition nor my willing and wanting can effect in any degree changes in body-Body. Positively, I shall assume that there are orders of telic beings each of which is to be defined in its own terms and to be related to each other as the evidence warrants. These three orders are the mental, the physiological, and the physico-chemical. I am purposely leaving the theoretical door open to hypotheses about para-psychological phenomena and religious experience.

A simple illustration may clarify the relational situation of the person. When I go to my optometrist to check my vision, he asks me to describe certain lines and colors projected on a screen before both of us. I report to him the results of my inspection. He has already put drops in my Body-Eyes which I experience as changes in my lived -body-eyes. These qualiative changes "in" my lived-body would not take place, I infer, without the changes in my Physiological Eye "produced" by the Chemical. There are two interacting sets of events going on, but I experience only the lived-eye-changes. Furthermore, the optometrist prescribes lenses for me in accordance with the norm of 20 -20 vision, and with what he knows about the Eye, the Optic Nerve, and with certain portions of the Brain--all of which I have never experienced qualiatively. But all of this Physico-Chemical scheme has been constructed by correlation with such experiences as persons like me undergo. Presumably the norm, 20-20 vision, is constructed from studies correlating experienced visual qualities with changes in the Physiological Organs as related to the Order of the Physical World. As my eye-examination goes on, the optometrist relates his non-lived, established constructions to the reports I give of my lived-condition. Let us say that he concludes that the changes I report indicate a change in my Physiological Eye consistent with changes in my Physiological History and that of other persons of my age in this kind of Physical Environment.

In eye-examination, then, three interacting orders are involved: (a) I and my lived-body as related to (b) my Body as the optometrist perceives and understands it, and (c), both (a) and (b) as related to the order of Physico-Chemical events as viewed by (an accepted consensus of) physical scientists. But the eye-glasses prescribed will be inadequate unless all three orders are related, and take into account my lived-visual-condition.

Accordingly, I have no reasonable ground for minimizing the need for hypothetical constructions concerning Orders other than those in my lived-body--in this instance constructions about the Biological and Physical Order that meet the data and facts of concern to investigators in these Realms. What I am protesting is that set of claims often made, alas, in the name of "science," that <u>all</u> the dimensions of personal being and experience can be understood as reflecting conditions in the biological and physical world. We must, of course, search for more specific relationships between the lived-body, the non-lived Body, and the Physical Order, but we cannot allow descriptions-explanations framed within the context of the physical, chemical, biological, and even of the social sciences to be final, especially if the person as he experiences himself has been disregarded to begin with.

G.   Reflective overview

Central to the interpretation of the person here proposed is the thesis that interpretations of the activity -potentials constitutive of his essentially conscious -selfconscious nature should not lose their grip on the quality and dynamics they are meant to clarify and explain. I suggested that the unity of the person, necessary to knowing succession as succession, is more reasonably interpreted as self-identifying and not as self-identical unity.

In order to understand better the inferred processes that occur during intermittency, I propose that the person's "margins" be extended by such purposive agency (mentality) as can be reasonably analogous with conscious-selfconscious activities. On this view, the unconscious of depth therapies, for example, is not alien to the self-identifying conscious person, since processes that take place therein are intelligible to the extent that they can be understood as analogous to, and related to, the goals of the person's conscious-selfconscious being-becoming.

Again, the person's experiences of the given varied orders of his lived-body become his initial bases for reasonably conceiving Realms of beings (the Physical, the Chemical, and the Biological, each with its own Order) and for relating them to the lived-body's changes and growth.

Generalizing, we can say that the clarifying and explanatory process by which the self-identifying being-becoming person understands himself and the course of his own development calls for his relating his activity-potentials to his lived -body, and in so doing also "constructing" the links to reasonably inferred Orders of being (interacting with which supports, threatens, and challenges his being-becoming in manifold ways).

We found adequate reasons for denying that the person's mental being is identified with his Body, however that Body is related to the vast non-mental, non-living Realms conceived by experts in the natural sciences. What should be clear is that questions about particular interactions of the person with the extra-personal Orders are left open for further theory and observation. Interaction is a mystery in the sense that any ultimate is--namely, it cannot be explained by any other kind of event: any attempt to do so re-introduces it (ultimacy). Thus, I affirm the interaction of personal activities with each other and with Body and Physical World without affirming how interactions take place. An adequately developed theory of the person requires an adequate theory of such "others."

As we shall see, when I inspect and interpret feeling and emoting as constitutive activities of the person, I shall seek to allow the conscious data to speak for themselves and never declare them "off bounds" because of some presupposed theory of Body and Physical World. Fuller explanation may well call for more than will be offered (owing largely to limitations in my knowledge). But it is not to minimize reliance upon Bodily and Physical knowledge to proceed with the determination to "save the appearances" that are lost from <u>adequate</u> account if these are not seen in their conscious context within the person's being-becoming. The conscious context is the necessary beginning for our investigation; it is by no means necessarily sufficient as we seek to understand its being and its <u>interrelations</u> with all we reasonably connect with it.

Notes for Chapter Three

1. Clarence I. Lewis, _Mind and the World-Order_ (New York:
    Scribner's Sons, 1929), 416.

2. See my "The Person and His Body: Critique of
    Existentialist Responses to Descartes," in _Cartesian
    Essays: A Collection of Critical Studies_, eds. Bernard
    Magnus and James B. Wilbur (The Hague: Nijhoff, 1969):
    and "Descartes and Marcel on the Person and His Body: A
    Critique," _Proceedings of the Aristotelian Society_, 68
    (1968).

3. See W. H. Werkmeister, "The World I Live In," _Mid
    -Twentieth Century American Philosophy: Personal
    Statements_, ed. Peter A. Bertocci (New York: Humanities
    Press, 1974), 227-239.

4. See an interesting parallel to this view (although
    explanations are different) in C. J. Ducasse's
    statement: "Just this, then, is the ultimate criterion
    of the `mental' or `psychical,' its _esse_ is its
    experiri, and the experiencing is the _intuent_
    experiencing." Ducasse also adds: "The psychical or
    mental, however, comprises not only intuings--all of
    which are cases of undergoing--but also cases of many
    kinds of _intentional_, _purposive_ doing, i.e. of
    acting..." _Brain and Mind_, ed. J. R. Smythies (London:

Routledge and Kegan Paul, 1965), 95. However, when Ducasse contends that a "mind is essentially a more or less well-integrated set of capacities, such as those just mentioned, only insofar as it has a history--its history being the series of such exercises as its capacities have had, are having, and will possibly have" (ibid., 81.), he presupposes an account of memory. As H. H. Price properly asks: "to count as a mind, must it not in some way `retain' at least part of the history which it has had up to now?" (ibid., 101.). It is to account for unity and continuity that I suggested the temporalistic view of the person in chapter One.

5. I note, in passing, that Herbert Feigl, who has struggled so hard to find a conceptualization of the identity-theory of mind and body, realizes that mental and bodily being cannot be strictly identified. "We have knowledge of the phenomenally given (the "raw feels" of sensation, desire, emotion, intention, etc.) by direct acquaintance; whereas our knowledge of physical objects (including our own brain) and the process in which they are involved...is indirect." See his essay, "No Pot of Message," Mid-Twentieth Century American Philosophy, ed. Peter A. Bertocci (New York: Humanities Press, 1974), 136. My concern is to show that if we take the meaning of objective reference and

of knowing seriously, there is no basis for the analogy that justifies granting to physiological and physical processes _qualities_ that are, as Feigl says, for us objects of immediate awareness. Mind and body simply cannot be understood as two perspectives of the same world, once we realize that one can make errors while the other cannot. There is something in one perspective that has _no_ analogy in the other, for a brain-state cannot make a mistake (that, as I say, presupposes objective referring). See my essay, "A Temporalistic View of Personal Mind," _Theories_ _of_ _the_ _Mind_, ed. Jordan Scher (New York: Free Press, 1962, 398-421).

6. Sir John Eccles, in _Facing_ _Reality_: _Philosophical_ _Adventures_ _of_ _a_ _Brain_ _Scientist_ (New York: Springer -Verlag, 1970), has provided us with an impressive set of essays recording his reasons for being unable to identify mind with brain, or to regard mind as an ineffectual by-product of brain-events. Marjorie Grene criticizes the dualism in Eccles' view and seeks to "naturalize" the differences between the personal, the biological, and the physical. But she neglects, I would say, the distinction I am pointing to between the cognitive situation and any other. (See her essay "People and Other Animals," _Philosophical_ _Forum_, 3 (1972):157-173.)

7. See Arthur Lovejoy, The Revolt against Dualism (La Salle, Illinois: Open Court, 1930).

8. I hardly need to follow Gilbert Ryle in accusing Descartes of holding to a ghost in the machine (see Gilbert Ryle, The Concept of Mind, 1949, especially chapter I), in order to suggest that Descartes' basic mistake was to assume that sensed qualia are all non -extended. If, like Descartes, I reason that my body is entirely to be understood as belonging to the non -mental, extended realm of nature, then like him I am tempted to consider the complete man as somehow united with the body. This view, however, does not live up to what I actually experience. If my counter-proposal is correct, while my lived-body is not obviously distinguishable from the total realm of sensory qualia and their refractory order, I soon find grounds for distinguishing it from that larger "world" of sensory qualia, and also for the conclusion that it both belongs to me and does not belong to me. This whole topic of mind and body, as well as the whole problem of the way in which we know our minds, is freshly treated in H. D. Lewis, The Self and Immortality (New York: Seabury Press, 1973), especially chapters 2-8.

9. See the interchange between C. J. Ducasse, H. H. Price, Lord Brain, and J. R. Smythies, in Brain and Mind, ed.

J. R. Smythies (London: Routledge and Kegan Paul, 1965).

10. See James M. Edie, "Descartes and the Phenomenological Problem of the Embodiment of Consciousness," with its specific references to Husserl and Sartre's response to Descartes, in Cartesian Essays: A Collection of Critical Studies, ed. Bernard Magnus and James W. Wilbur (The Hague: Nijhoff, 1969), 91-116.)

11. In his essay, "The Limits of Naturalism," (Contemporary American Philosophy (Second Series), ed. John E. Smith (New York: Humanities Press, 1970), Brand Blanshard shows the bankruptcy of such views. I have already referred to the work of H. D. Lewis and of C. J. Ducasse (see Nature, Mind, and Death especially) as other excellent critiques. See also Milic Capek, "The Main Difficulties of the Identity Theory," in Scientia, 63 (1969). In Facing Reality: Philosophical Adventures by a Brain Scientist (New York: Springer-Verlag, 1970), Sir John Eccles expounds a view that is consonant with what is suggested here. (See also the "dialogue" between Eccles and Karl Popper, The Self and its Brain (New York: Springer-Verlag, 1977.)

CHAPTER FOUR

Feeling: Its Nature and Content

A.   Terminological uncertainties

We all agree that feelings and emotions play an important part in human life. What distinctive part(s)? Straightway we become aware of the variety, let alone ambiguities, in our everyday usage of the terms--by no means removed by scholarly analyses of the nature of feeling and emotion and of the difference they make to knowing and behaving. In 1937, William McDougall began his monograph, The Organization of the Affective Life. A Critical Survey, with the words: "The psychology of the affective life is still so backward, so chaotic, there is so much diversity of opinion and of theory, that we have no approach to a generally accepted terminology."[1] In 1965, Edward J. Murray, noting at the beginning of Motivation and Emotion that there was some question as to whether motivation and emotion are different areas, goes on to say that some psychologists "would eliminate motivation and emotion entirely as a topic for general psychology" since "they regard the subject as the last refuge of the humanists, the vitalists, and teleologists."[2] That the situation among other psychologists was still no different in 1970 is clear from the essays in Feelings and Emotions, edited by Magda Arnold.[3] They indicate that the terminological uncertainties that prevail are the effect of different conceptions of the task of psychological science, of the ideal of truth, and of other related issues. Hence the attempt here to defend a view of feeling that distinguishes it as an activity-potential of the person is not a little sobered by the knotty difficulties underlying the bewildering variety of the everyday and the more critical usage of "feeling."

B.   Quandaries that are more than terminological

1. In the passage quoted above, McDougall speaks not about feelings and emotions, but about "the affective life." He does not stand outside an extensive tradition when he "roughly and broadly" uses "affective" to denote "all the factors of mental life other than the cognitive or intellectual."[4] Rough and broad as usage is, we cannot disregard a frequent assumption that what a person knows at

all by way of feeling is extraordinary and exclusive in some respect.

Nevertheless, what seems so often to be intended is that our experiences of pleasantness and unpleasantness, in whatever broader, experiental context, are states of ourselves that do not as such convey truth or falsity about something beyond themselves. Indeed, "the affective life" becomes an omnibus term that includes "willing," "aesthetic," "moral," and "religious" responses, especially when these are assumed to be essentially noncognitive. It even includes what many call the "conative" life, the presumably noncognitive experiences of striving, such as impulses, desires, wants, and emotions.

2. Even this brief reference to the varied uses of "feeling" serves to warn us of the porous vessels that they are. How often, for example, is "feeling" used to indicate a matrix of awareness that we cannot "pin-point" otherwise. Thus we often hear psychologists and psychotherapists, moralists, artists, theologians, and metaphysicans say that feeling is the bedrock of our lives, from which other more specific states and functions arise.[5] Yet, to speak of "the life of feeling" in this way allows all kinds of presuppositions to receive authenticity that resists further warrant. One may well ask: If "life" is not thought, if it is not sense, if it is not x or y, is it illuminating to say that it is feeling, unless we can specify what we mean by "feeling

-consciousness" as opposed, say, to color-consciousness or to thought-consciousness? Should we not set aside both the notion of a reservoir of relatively simple and amorphous affective sensitivity from which varied feelings and emotions flow, and also the supposition that relatively primitive and undifferentiated sensitivity can indeed illuminate what persons who have symbolic and varied cognitive capacities undergo? Surely, every attempt to identify "feeling(s)" and "emotion(s)" in pre-selfconscious experience presupposes what qualities of experiences we take these terms to capture in our self-conscious experience. 3. Once more, our presuppositions about the nature of knowledge generally, and about approaches to understanding persons, are at work; and nowhere is it more important to be aware of what they are. Consistent with the method and criterion of knowledge I have been using, I propose that, whatever other approaches we take to understanding what is involved in feelings and emotions, we begin by inspecting them as experienced, with a view to knowing, for example, what qualities of experience would be left out if we lost our capacity to experience them. When I speak of inspecting, I am not assuming a special way of "knowing from within" (introspection) that has privileged status, or that is in every way different from a presumed way of knowing what is "outside" me, since that separation is not as such experienced. I refer only to the claim that I, a person, am aware of what I am consciously experiencing. This qualitative awareness--what it refers to, for example--is always open to further investigation. Indeed, since presumably introspected (inspected) experiences are often not what they were taken to be, I cannot but concur when someone says "You cannot trust introspection." But I reply: "I cannot know that without introspecting." Or, if someone says: "But introspection is always retrospection, so you can't `capture' present awareness," I reply, "Is not this claim itself the result of present inspection?" In any case, once we are aware of the dangers of relying on inspection, it seems simply wrong-headed to give up a possible source of knowledge that is so distinctively available to persons.

4.I am not arguing, then, that statements based on inspection have complete authority in ascertaining truth either about myself or about my relation to other minds and the world. Any seemingly "obvious" claims, any "psychological certitudes," are subject to further analysis and inspection. It may turn out that I am a "moment" of God's experience or the by-product of electro-chemical changes in the brain.

Nevertheless, in order to make up for the "errors of introspection" we should not substitute for conscious experience what may well be a condition of it. For example, it is often argued that feelings and emotions are nothing but certain bio-chemical processes. If so, how is it known that such bio-chemical processes involve "anger" rather than "fear," "sympathy" rather than "respect," without prior description of the conscious experiences? It is one thing to say that there are bio-chemical correlates of our conscious feelings and emotions; it is another to identify such experiences with them. It was the great psysiologist, Charles S. Sherrington, who said: "For myself, what little I know of the how of the one [brain processes] does not, speaking personally, even begin to help me toward the how of the other [conscious experiences]. The two for all I can do remain refractorily apart. They seem to me disparate; not mutually convertible; untranslatable the one into the other."[6]

In the last analysis, then, each of us must accept the responsiblility for his own descriptions of what seems to be taking place in his conscious experience, and all the more remain open to the corrections that come from discussion with others. I shall follow the method and criterion of truth suggested as I venture to inspect and interpret the experiences of feeling.

C.   The experience of pleasantness and
         unpleasantness

The only way I know to avoid the omnibus use of the term feeling (or affective) is to restrict it to the experiences

of pleasantness and unpleasantness. I do not oppose
"pleasantness" to "pain" because I take it that pain is
essentially sensory experience, despite the varied
unpleasant experiences that usually go with pains.[7] I shall
often substitute the use of the terms `hedonic tone' and
`unhedonic tone' for "pleasant" and "unpleasant"
respectively to emphasize the qualitative variety actually
experienced.

The view that I shall defend is rooted in experiences of
the following kind. I am looking at two neckties, one red
and the other blue. As I shift my gaze from one to the
other, I experience the different hedonic tone of each. In
this experience I note that red and that blue are pleasant
in distinctive ways--not just pleasant, or one more pleasant
than the other. It may occur to me, at first glance at
least, that the hedonic tone experienced is not the
particular, hedonic tone of each color. Indeed, in this
experience, while I may characterize each color as pleasant,
it is only when I pay close attention that I realize that
the hedonic tone of red is not identical with that of blue.
Moreover, I remember occasions when I have regarded them
each as unhedonic. But I doubt that I could ever displace
red by blue without experiencing some difference in hedonic
tone, however little it may be.

Again, I am listening to the musical notes in a Chopin
piano concerto. Each sound is different; the sounds are

those of a particular piano, and the rendition is that of a particular pianist. As I listen, I experience the particular hedonic tones of those sounds in their patterns. In other circumstances these sounds-in-pattern would be experienced with difference in hedonic tone. I cannot find words to express the differences, but I know that they occur, and I may be even "offended" when a less accomplished pianist plays the concerto, since I can discriminate differences in hedonic tone as I discriminate the differences in the sounds. Hedonic tones, therefore, occur as distinguishable experiences, as "brute qualities" in my experience; and my stipulative words do not begin to capture all the nuances. However I may finally explain the occurrence of particular hedonic tones--to what extent, for example, their occurrence is a joint product of myself and my environment--I cannot but conclude that I never experience hedonic tone as such, independently of some experienced object.

So far I have been underscoring a basic point Magda Arnold makes: "The distinction between pleasantness and unpleasantness, touch and pain, hunger and love as different kinds of experience is primary; they are felt directly and need no intermediary knowledge of pressure patterns."[8] Since I shall be unable to agree with other aspects of Arnold's view of pleasantness and unpleasantness, I set out the crucial point and important consequences.

Pleasantness or unpleasantness (hedonic and unhedonic tone) simply do not exist as such. This is, in fact, a ground for my earlier protest against the omnibus use of "feeling." What we experience are feelings, hedonic tones that we try to tease out of our total experience at any moment, even though our words cannot begin to keep up with the variety of feelings.

2. When it is proposed that persons must seek pleasure, or a maximum of pleasantness over unpleasantness, we should press the question: Which hedonic quality, or pattern of hedonic tones, is intended? It is hardly illuminating for me to say that I choose pleasure as the goal of life without noting which pleasure(s). For pleasure (so-called) is always "attached to" something other than itself. The taste of the coffee I just brewed has a different hedonic tone from that of the cup left over from the morning. I prefer the hedonic tone of this coffee-taste (which I may interpret as the byproduct of what is in the brew and of my psycho -physiological nature at this point). Hence, we may use the terms, pleasant, unpleasant, hedonic and unhedonic tone, as universals that refer to similarities in our experiences, but we do not experience similarities as such but only the specific experiences with their hedonic tones.

3. The very blue that I find so pleasant in one context may be unpleasant in another. From this fact it may be inferred that "pleasantness" and "unpleasantness" do not characterize

the "object" (blue), but characterize me (as knowing subject). This probably is the reason for the claim that pleasantness and unpleasantness are subjective states and not properties of the object. But this statement calls for further interpretation.

The actual fact is that the hedonic experience bespeaks the object in relation to me. When I am in a different frame of mind, the same blue color may indeed be experienced as a different hedonic tone, but the brute quality of that different hedonic tone in my experience will not be denied --in this instance as a byproduct of that object-blue and my total state. Accordingly, while we can say that the hedonic tone is an individual matter, there is no justification for the conclusion that pleasantness and unpleasantness are "purely subjective"--as if we could experience that hedonic pattern at will. Yet, as F. R. Tennant said: "That feeling is evoked, must be affirmed, because its emergence makes no alteration in the object cognised, whereas change of object does occasion change in feeling."[9]

I need not commit myself on the exact referent of "object"--whether, for example, it includes interaction with an existent beyond the experience that the experient knows as blue. The important consideration here is that the hedonic tone is related, but not confined, to the sensory (or other) experienced content. Even more important, for the quality of our experience as persons, is this fact that our sensory data (however they are finally interpreted) are phases of what I may call a total "appreciative" experience. Who envies a camera that can "record" blue but never experiences pleasant or unpleasant? A day gleaming in sunlight makes a qualitative hedonic difference to our lives; a damp, sunless day may indeed dampen our spirits. Such hedonic responses are facts about persons.

Hence, I concur with the drift of Paul Ricoeur's comment: "Specific, localized, and infinitely diversified pleasure, the pleasure of a thousand nuances, actually maintains complex relations with the senses: it is a pleasure of the senses, engendered in a sensation, gratuitous as all that is encountered and received. In this respect we are no more authors of our pleasures than of our pains."[10] Particular hedonic and unhedonic tones are as refractory as _experienced_ as is our experience of blue; we can "create" neither at will. (As later discussion will reveal, non-sensory experiences, such as emotions, are experienced as hedonic, with variations dependent on context.)

It may well be that pleasant experiences often have survival value, but an experience does not become pleasant simply because it has survival value. I here reluctantly disagree with the view advanced by Magda Arnold to whose work I owe so much. Independent attention to her two volumes, _Emotion and Personality_, is indispensable, and will here serve to show how theoretical differences at some points influence the interpretation of experience at others.

D.   Is feeling a consequence of appraisal?

1. Basic to Arnold's view of feeling is that feelings are sui generis. Feelings are neither reducible to, nor derivative from, sensations; nor are they to be identified with emotions. They are not the elements from which emotions are built. As she observes: "Feelings of great pleasantness, considerable excitement, and some strain still do not add up to the emotion of joy."[11] Moreover, feeling pleasantness and unpleasantness varies independently of the emotion; one and the same emotion can be either pleasant or unpleasant. This welcome refusal to lump together feeling and emotion, or make either omnibus terms, is supported by Arnold's evaluation of an extensive relevant literature.

2. What gives me serious pause about Arnold's own theory of feeling (and emotion) involves controversial epistemic questions--particularly whether feelings and emotions are ways of knowing. Her essential thesis is that cognitive appraisal is intrinsic to each; and this is part of a larger theory of knowledge. She sums up: "Organic sensations as well as external sensations provide information about things (including our body), while feelings indicate how things affect us."[12]

In contrast to this claim, I have argued that although hedonic tones are experienced involuntarily, they do not as such give us any assured, independent information about ourselves or the world. Arnold, however, goes so far as to say: "Feelings assess what is there."[13] What underlies her view and mine are theories of knowledge. Too much is at stake not to pause for further analysis.

3. Arnold's epistemic view is clearly stated: "When we see, we do not see a sensation (or light waves) but a thing."[14] "If the only direct experiences we have are experiences of some thing, this must mean that the object is not inferred but is directly given."[15] However, the object, be it a stone or our bodies, is never known by any single sensory function. So, in classical Aristotelian-Thomistic realistic fashion, Arnold hypothesizes a common sense to integrate the different sensory qualities, as afforded by each sensory function.

Underlying this historic, realistic contention is the conviction that skepticism is entailed by any other view of sensory-perceptual experience. As she herself puts it, to affirm that "we only know sensations, not objects, contradicts our common-sense experience and forces us into paradoxes from which there is no escape: we know only sensations, not objects, but sensations cannot be directly known because they are constructs..."[16] To avert such disaster, she insists, "our data must be the things we experience in our commerce with the world outside us."[17]

My rejoinder builds on contentions already advanced (especially in discussing knowledge of our bodies). The postulation of an integrative common sense in addition to our sensory functions does not guaranteee the particular kind of objectivity Arnold ascribes to the senses in order to ground our knowledge of the world, including our bodies. After all, the objects in our dreams would require the integration of the sensory qualities that we attribute to them. But would they cease to be dream-things?

The underlying bone of contention is the interpretation of our experience of objective reference. I suggest that we should interpret this experience with the data of sensory-perceptual errors, illusions, and dreams in mind. I have pressed the fact that our sensory qualities do not come with labels on them--even those of our own body.

Indeed, our initial sensory experiences are not tagged "sensory." The existence of error leads me to deny that the experience of objective reference in itself justifies the conclusion that what is thus experienced is knowledge of what is indeed referred to. Nor can I grant that the only alternative left by this denial is a thorough-going skepticism. After all, the refractoriness in our sensory experience, interpreted reasonably in connection with other considerations, does take us to a probable account of our

Bodies and of our World that we can trust--always as a basis for further thought and action.

E.   Does the experience of hedonic tone presuppose appraisal?

1. Fortunately, this difference in theory of knowledge does not disturb the thesis that feeling-experience and sense -experience are not the same. But the following passage puts succinctly Arnold's additional contention that in feeling as well as in sensory experience we acquire information, albeit different, about what is referred to. "If the only direct experiences we have are experiences of some thing, this must mean that the object is not inferred but is directly given... The introspective report would be: this thing is there. And feeling would be the direct experience of some object as it affects me via some sense modality. The introspective report would be: This is pleasant or unpleasant."[18]

I take this passage and others to mean that the direct awareness of hedonic tone is also direct knowledge about the object given by means of sensory functions. However, I would not experience hedonic tone as the qualification of some sensory or non-sensory qualities unless some appraisal has already taken place. "Pleasant" and "unpleasant," therefore, indicate something about the world and in its

relation to me. What is that? Arnold's answer is that the
blue object, for example, is "favorable" (if experienced as
pleasant), or "unfavorable" (if experienced as unpleasant).
"The evidence does show that pleasantness is experienced
when something affects us favorably, unpleasantness when
something affects us adversely."[19]

2. What judgment can we render at this point? Apart from
epistemic issues already discussed, I must wonder at
Arnold's conclusion that pleasant, as experienced,
presupposes the appraisal "favorable" ("unpleasant" an
unfavorable appraisal). For hedonic tone is hedonic tone,
unhedonic tone is unhedonic tone, even as blue and red, as
experienced, are what they are. That "pleasant" is
favorable for something other than itself is not given.
When we use "favorable" we add "for." But we do not require
"for" when we affirm: "The blue book is pleasant." Yet on
Arnold's view to know the blue book as pleasant is to know
it also as favorable for the experient. But blue book, I
suggest, is prima facie neither favorable nor unfavorable,
insofar as its hedonic tone is experienced.

In any case, Arnold's interpretation faces an independent
difficulty. For, if hedonic experience involves favorable
for, then the criterion for favorable needs to be supplied.
This criterion is surely not given as part of "the blue
object," or "the pleasant blue object." We do not know
whether, given pleasant blue object, we thereby also know

that it will indeed be favorable for us in some respect or other. Nor will our preference for an hedonically toned blue presuppose knowledge that it will be favorable.

3. To summarize: Pleasantness and unpleasantness, if I am correct, are variable hedonic qualities that we discriminate in our conscious experience as concomitants of sensory qualities, and of non-sensory processes (such as wanting and emoting). Our words never catch the particularity of an hedonic quality, or pattern of hedonic qualities. Yet each hedonic tone is, I submit, an irreducible, specific given that disappears when the object or process it appears to qualify ceases to be. This irreducibility, however, cannot be taken to mean that the hedonic tone, when it appears, is the simple consequent of the sensory or non -sensory events, taken in abstraction from the total state of the conscious person. Thus far there is no disagreement with Arnold.

But I would protect the cognitive "innocence" of hedonic qualities. In holding that hedonic tones are innocent, I am urging that they are qualities which are not what they are because they are interpreted, or rest on some appraisal. It seems clear to me that the particular hedonic tone I experience, say in my awareness of a red apple that I perceive, is pleasant because of my desiring the experiences it gives me as I eat it, or is pleasant because of the sensed color and shape, or both. I am affirming that the hedonic and unhedonic tones are not known, to begin with, as favorable or unfavorable "for." "Pleasant" and "favorable" are not synonyms.

4. This verdict, that hedonic tone does not in itself presuppose or reflect appraisal or evaluation, has consequences both for theory of human motivation and of values. If I am correct, we do not initially prefer pleasant experience to unpleasant experience because of some estimative judgment, for instance, that pleasant experiences are favorable for survival. It cannot be assumed that what makes survival valuable (or good) is its hedonic quality. Indeed, what makes hedonic qualities "good" or "bad" involves larger issues, such as deciding the norm for "good" or "bad." If we conclude that survival as survival is the standard of good, then we need to know whether hedonic or unhedonic experiences in fact always support survival, and, if so, which hedonic tones are more trustworthy guides to this goal. Hence the claim that men do, or ought to, live "for pleasure" is one hardly supported by the claim here made that our experience as persons would be unrecognizable without the hedonic tones which saturate it. For, by themselves, hedonic tones as such do not constitute the standard of the good life.

F.   The relation of feeling and wants

1. Having focussed on the relation of hedonic tones to
sensory experience, we must now consider the relation of
hedonic tone to the wanting or striving (conative)
dimensions of experience. We note, to begin with, that as
any tension (any impulse, want, desire, urge) is being
relieved, and to the extent that it is relieved, we
experience hedonic tone. What calls for particular notice
is the fact that the gratification of (or frustration of)
any particular want brings its own (quality of) hedonic
tone. The hedonic quality one experiences in gratifying
thirst is not the same as that resulting from gratifying
hunger. Indeed, the actual quality of the hedonic tone
will depend both upon the nature of the want and upon the
nature of the gratifying factor--for example, upon the water
or coffee that relieves thirst, or upon the foods that
relieve hunger, or upon the thought that gratifies wonder.

Thus is confirmed our earlier conclusion that hedonic
tone is not dependent on the object or the subject alone but
on the factors involved in the situation experienced. A
very thirsty man, for example, may find it pleasantly
gratifying to drink almost any liquid; he may drink what is
not healthful for him--as when shipwrecked persons, who have
been drifting for days, may finally drink, with immediate
relish, the salt water that may be fatal. Again, the week

-end fisherman takes pleasure more in the mackerel he caught than in the catch as such. In such situations the total process of experiencing and gratifying a particular want by way of this particular object has the hedonic quality unique to it. Both subjective and objective factors are involved in producing the hedonic state that emerges as joint product in that situation. Is it not the case that the wanting factor is also involved in producing the final quality of the hedonic tone?

2. These considerations by themselves help us to see why the claim is false that persons must seek pleasure. A person is not activated by such a goal to begin with. He often wants this and that even before he knows what the quality of hedonic tone will be; and he certainly does not know the yield of pleasantness and unpleasantness in complex patterns, or how to evaluate them in relation to other factors in his life.[20] The fact that persons do easily become motivated by quantities or qualities of pleasure does not mean that pleasure is itself an independent, basic motive to which all further motives and actions conform.

G.   The distinction between higher and lower
     pleasures

Is there any justification in hedonic experience themselves for our speaking of "higher" or "lower" pleasures? Certainly no hedonic tone in itself comes labelled "higher." But if, as we have seen, hedonic tone is a joint product of the objective and the subjective in the agent's life, then a particular joint product, say, poetry -pleasure, may be termed "higher" or "lower" than ping-pong pleasure. Poetry-hedonic-tone is not ping-pong-hedonic -tone, and no amount or quantity of the one will produce the other. The experienced difference may enter into final evaluations of higher and lower values, but the difference in hedonic tone in a specific context does not in itself suffice to produce the higher evaluation. Again, we can say that experiencing a sunset has intrinsic hedonic tone, as does experiencing a sonata, but the sonata-hedonic-tone may be held by an experient to be higher than that sunset -hedonic-tone because he esteems that total sonata -experience to be more valuable than that sunset-experience in the light of his criterion of the good.

I am urging that final evaluation may well rest on the person's assessment of the part any hedonically-toned experience will play in his life in the light of the variety and conflict between many hedonically-toned experiences, let alone other values he acknowledges. Accordingly, without denying prima facie differences in the quality of hedonic tones, we cannot on the ground of such differences alone estimate their normative ethical value.

H.   Reflective overview

Hedonic and unhedonic tones are experienced as brute, qualitatively different data that are not reducible to--nor add up to--the sensory and conative (and other) experiences they accompany. They are always experienced in a matrix they qualify; but no conative or cognitive experience "owns" a particular hedonic tone regardless of the matrix, even though we may speak of the "characteristic" hedonic tone of certain "objects" and "experiences."

In view of this conclusion, we may now think of the self -identifying person as the complex unity of activity -potentials whose expression and actualization, from within and in commerce with Environment, are laden with hedonic tones. These hedonic tones in themselves must be taken into account in speaking of what it means _for_ _a_ _person_ to survive, let alone to survive with quality. But this does not mean that hedonic tones, important as they are in the choices they influence, are themselves the product of some estimative function. Inescapable factors in defining the nature and range of personal responses, hedonic qualities take their place at this stage in our study as accompaniments of the varied activities constituting personal being-becoming. We have said that hedonic tones do not make up wants and emotions but that they influence the

course of the expression of wants and emotions. Until we
are clearer about the nature of "wants and emotions" this
judgment will leave much to be desired as to the dynamics of
feelings, wants, and emotions in the given constitution and
development of the person.

Notes for Chapter Four

1. William McDougall, <u>The</u> <u>Organization</u> <u>of</u> <u>the</u> <u>Affective</u>
   <u>Life</u>. <u>A</u> <u>Critical</u> <u>Survey</u>. Reprinted from <u>Acta</u>
   <u>Psychologica</u>, vol. 2 (3, March, 1937): 233-346.

2. Edward Murray, Jr., <u>Motivation</u> <u>and</u> <u>Emotion</u>, 3rd ed.
   (New York: Prentice Hall, 1965), vi. See also Paul
   Thomas Young, <u>Motivation</u> <u>and</u> <u>Emotion</u> (New York: Wiley
   and Sons, 1961), viii.

3. Magda B. Arnold, ed. <u>Feelings</u> <u>and</u> <u>Emotions</u> (New York:
   Academic Press, 1970). See also <u>The</u> <u>Nature</u> <u>of</u> <u>Emotion</u>:
   <u>Selected</u> <u>Readings</u>, ed. Magda B. Arnold (Baltimore,
   Maryland: Penguin Books, 1968).

4. McDougall, ibid., 233.

5. In her fascinating work, <u>Mind</u>: <u>An</u> <u>Essay</u> <u>on</u> <u>Feeling</u>
   (Baltimore: Johns Hopkins Press, 1967), Susanne Langer
   succumbs, I suggest, to this loose use of the term
   albeit for her own reasons. See my essay, "Susanne K.
   Langer's Theory of Feeling and Mind," <u>Review</u> <u>of</u>
   <u>Metaphysics</u>, 13 (3, March, 1970): 527-551. Readers of
   William James and of Alfred North Whitehead will
   recognize similar ambiguity, alongside of very specific
   meaning, in usage. See also F. Krueger's appeal to
   recognize the "feeling-like" character of our experience
   as "total-whole," in "The Essence of Feeling," in <u>The</u>
   <u>Nature</u> <u>of</u> <u>Emotion</u>, ed. M. B. Arnold (Baltimore,
   Maryland: Penguin Books, 1968).

6. Charles S. Sherrington, Man on His Nature, 2d. ed. (New York: Doubleday Anchor Books, 1953), 252, and see 244, 245.

7. R. Melzak and K. L. Casey conclude: "Pain varies along both sensory-discriminative and motivational-affective dimensions. The magnitude along these dimensions, moreover, is influenced by cognitive activities, such as evaluation of the seriousness of the injury... anxiety or anguish without somatic input is not pain. Pain must be defined in terms of its sensory, motivational, and central control determinants." "The Affective Dimension of Pain", in Feelings and Emotions, ed. Magda Arnold, 65.

8. Magda B. Arnold, Emotion and Personality, vol. 1 (New York: Columbia University Press, 1960), 41.

9. Frederick R. Tennant, Philosophical Theology, vol. 1 (Cambridge: Cambridge University Press, 1928), 25.

10. Paul Ricoeur, Freedom and Nature: The Voluntary and the Involuntary, tr. E. V. Kohak (Evanston, Illinois: Northwestern University Press, 1966), 100.

11. Magda B. Arnold, Emotion and Personality, vol. 1 (New York: Columbia University Press, 1960, 24. For a good statement of the philosophical psychology involved in her work, see The Human Person: An Approach to an Integral Theory of Personality, ed. Magda B. Arnold and John A. Gasson, in collaboration with other scholars (New York: Ronald Press, 1954).

12. Magda B. Arnold, <u>Emotion</u> <u>and</u> <u>Personality</u>, vol. 1 (New York: Columbia University Press, 1960), 31.

13. Ibid., 8.

14. Ibid., 47.

15. Ibid., 50.

16. Ibid., 48.

17. Ibid.

18. Ibid., 50.

19. Ibid., 61.

20. See Silvio Arieti, "Cognition and Feeling," in <u>Feelings</u> <u>and</u> <u>Emotions</u>, ed. Magda Arnold.

CHAPTER FIVE

Considerations Basic to a Theory of Emotions in Persons

A.   The challenge to unify emotions and motives

Emotion! One word for a baffling variety of experiences. Our emotion-words do not begin to capture the differences in the emotive states we undergo. Of course, we face a similar poverty of terms for the differences in sensory experience, but in the sensory area we help ourselves often by finding something in our common world that enables us to signify some of the differences. For example, we stipulate one shade of "blue" as navy-blue, another as robin's egg-blue, and so on. But our words for distinguishing "an" emotion still embrace it in a rough and ready way--as a blanket does a kitten that scrambles here and there under it. I am too aware when I say, to take a simple instance, "I am angry," "I am getting angry," "I am quite angry," "I am purple with rage," that there is a distance between my words and the qualitative state I am undergoing and trying to convey.

The discussion of "feeling(s)" in the last chapter will support my stress here. Even when we have a word for different "emotional states," we must not delude ourselves into supposing that we are drawing neat circles around experiences. It is evident that feelings, wants, and emotions, for all the ambiguity that our linguistic use betrays, are somehow linked. What I shall suggest is a theory of motivation that accords with the motives of persons as they are experienced, a theory that will recognize such emotions as are themselves the actual constitutive motives (primary emotions) of persons. Over the years I have been gripped by the growing realization that from every quarter--biology, sociology, history, psychology, the arts, religion, and philosophy--we keep hearing of the great part that feelings, emotions, and unlearned motives play in the dynamics of change and growth. Nevertheless, verbal problems aside, we remain in the dark as to their relation.

Savour the vivid passage of William James, as he depicts the importance of emotions per se and as motives. "Conceive yourself, if possible, suddenly stripped of all the emotion with which your world now inspires you, and try to imagine it as it exists, purely by itself, without your favourable or unfavourable, hopeful or apprehensive comment... No one portion of the universe would then have importance beyond another; and the whole significance of its things and series of its events would be without significance, character, expression, or perspective.... The passion of love is the most familiar and extreme example of this fact.... So with fear, with indignation, jealousy, ambition, worship. If they are there, life changes!"[1] Six decades later Charles Winckelmans de Cléty writes in existentialist-phenomenological vein: "It is a matter of experience that, at every moment, the concrete way in which my surroundings exist for me depends very much on my mood, on my particular affective disposition. My room-for-me joyful is not the same reality as my room-for-me depressed.... The moon in the sky does not shine for me in the same way when I am worried and when I am at peace."[2]

There is no doubt that our lives would be "dead," "dull," "empty," without the difference made by "emotion" and "emotional states." But the moment we try to pin-point, let alone communicate, what these differences are, we find ourselves retreating to the vacuous generality, the omnibus term, "emotion." And then we find ourselves saying, with others, that there is in our lives some "bedrock" of feeling and emotion, of which our varied feelings and emotions are differentiations.

B.   Are neurological and behavioral indices adequate for identifying emotions?

1. The uncertainties ordinary mortals encounter in identifying emotions challenge some scholars to ground the distinctions they make in their words by referring to physiological states. For example, the psychologist, Karl H. Pribham, begins by distinguishing feelings as "monitors" from emotions as "plans." The emotions occur when "neural programs...are engaged when the organism is disequilibrated."[3] But immediately we wonder what the criterion of disequilibration is, and, moreover, whether it can be defined without reference to emotions and feelings as experienced.

But overlooking this fault, can we go on to say as Pribham does: "We feel hungry or sleepy or sexy. We feel happy or sad, contemplative or assertive"? Can the word "feeling" (rather than "emotion") grasp the qualitative differences we ourselves experience in "feeling happy or sad" and "feeling sexy"? There is much to be gained from Pribham's work, but we would certainly need to know why he assembles under the word "feeling" such different experienced states as "feelings of hunger, thirst, and sexiness; feelings of salience, of right and wrong" --granted that we should study such experienced states in terms of "neuroanatomical, neurophysical and neurobehavioral makeup."[4]

2. The exasperation caused by the disagreement of introspective accounts should indeed keep us seeking for objective ways of reducing it. But the way out does not seem to be any approach that fails to keep steadily before it human emotions as experienced in their quality and variety. I quote a passage from R. S. Peters that will illustrate the need to keep this experiential requirement in mind when an appeal to _linguistic use_ is made. "The phrases in which the terms `emotion' and its derivatives are not only natural but also almost indispensable as when we speak of judgments being disturbed, clouded, or warped by emotion, of people as being not properly in control of their emotions, being subject to gusts of emotion, being emotionally perturbed, upset, involved, excited, biased, and exhausted.... `Emotion,' in the standard use of the term rather than in that coined by philosophers and psychologists, is used to suggest mists on our mental windscreen rather than straightforward judgments..."[5]

The passage is simplistic. By what criterion does one distinguish the philosophical and psychological uses from the "standard uses?" By what logic does one then proceed to trust the standard used for reanalysis (by a philosophical psychologist in this instance)? The author here clearly supports his own introspection "by standard usage" and then proceeds to improve upon the account. In any case, the conclusions are equally damaging. To be sure, some emotional states are often characterized by negative reactions. But to say that this is the life of emotion is to allow the word "emotion" to stand for "impending" psychological, behavioral, or conceptual responses--without even attempting to ask: Is the range of our emotive experiences thus restricted?

C.   Will Plutchik's biological model serve to distinguish primary emotions?

1. Robert Plutchik favors an objective approach to emotions on the grounds that it is a "commonplace of clinical practice" that "many emotional states are not conscious."[6] Two pages later, he adds that "an individual may `have' an emotion and not be aware of it." Does this not earn John T. MacCurdy's rejoinder: "To speak about an emotion that is not conscious--for example, of fear of which one is not aware--is like speaking about pain of which one is unaware"?[7] If we hold that in principle the description of conscious emotions is not dependable, on what base shall we ground our differentiation of emotions to begin with?

2. To be sure, Plutchik holds that "it is unlikely that any one would question the statement that emotions differ from one another introspectively, that sorrow, for example, feels

different from anger."[8] Hence, he grants that "introspections may be useful in providing additional insights into the internal stimuli associated with certain adaptive reactions."[9] However, our problem comes to the fore again when Plutchik tries to fit emotions as introspected to the "adaptive reactions" that he accepts as the guide to his theory of primary emotions.

Plutchik makes his criterion of primary emotions unmistakable: "Whatever is taken to be a primary emotion should be applicable, in some sense, to lower evolutionary levels."[10] Since not even the higher animals have a range of emotions that corresponds to the human, this criterion forces us to rule out many human emotions that, as experienced qualitatively, are very important to persons. Nevertheless, Plutchik resorts to his alternative of referring emotions to some kinds of basic, "adaptive devices in the struggle for individual survival at all evolutionary levels."[11]

These adaptive devices "represent the eight prototypic dimensions of emotion: incorporation, rejection, destruction, protection, reproduction, deprivation, orientation, and exploration. These basic dimensions apply to all organismic levels from the lowest up to man. The terms used to describe them refer to overt behavior patterns or involve concepts like pleasure and pain which are definable in terms of overt behavior."[12]

To comment: it is obvious that in none of these dimensions is there a word that would usually itself be considered the name of an emotion. We are back here at the difficulty of identifying similarities of patterns of emotions in both animals and man. Do "underlying constancies in motor innervation...convey a universal meaning not only within, but also between vertebrate species"[13] <u>unless</u> the behavioral situations are already interpreted as having some purpose?

3. Indeed, Plutchik is aware that there is this problem of assigning an emotion to a pattern of behavior without an initial appeal to human introspection and the consequent correlation with observation and interpretation of particular adaptive patterns of behavior. His answer, however, is that the scientific method of discovering emotional states without reference to introspective reports may well require theoretical constructs that "do not necessarily have to accord with common sense so long as the experiences of common sense can ultimately be derived from them."[14] In Plutchik's theory, this means that there must be some analogy which allows us to see the tie between the hypothetical "ideal" construct and the adaptive behavioral pattern. That is, we ought to be able to find our way from the "ideal" construct and the adaptive behavioral pattern-- say, for example, from the "ideal" construct of sexual

emotion, or of anger, as correlated presumably with the adaptive pattern--to the common sense experience.

But two questions arise. If the behavior between species is admittedly so different, where, among the species, shall we look for the "ideal" construct of emotion with some hope of relevance to the range of emotions in persons? How can we make any contact with common sense if even common sense introspection is not there to guide the correlation of behavioral patterns with the conscious experience of primary emotions?

I must confess to some amazement, then, as Plutchik makes his transition to "expression of prototypic patterns in higher animals," that he can say: "It is generally evident with what emotions in man most of the prototypic patterns may be identified."[15] For, presumably, his prototypic pattern is constructed hypothetically as an ideal pattern hopefully applying to every species in the evolutionary scale. But surely there are qualities of emotions experienced by persons that would now be rather arbitrarily excluded as primary because there is no reliable guide in behavioral or neural pattern.

And I keep wondering how Plutchik (or any of us), without appeal to introspection, can know that "the destruction pattern would be associated with anger, the protection pattern with fear, the rejection pattern with disgust, the deprivation pattern with sorrow, the reproduction pattern with joy, and the incorporation pattern with acceptance."[16] Surely, these correlations are guided by introspection of emotion as related to a pattern of behavior interpreted ideally as performing a universal function! But it would seem that the meaning of the human emotion is now to be understood, at whatever final cost to immediate experience and reasonable correlations with bodily context, in terms of the behavior interpreted as adaptive. Yet the evaluative differentiation of adaptive from unadaptive function is not supplied in this evolutionary view. In any case, the basic question remains: Is the adaptive function, that an emotion may (or may not) have, a part of our actual experience of the emotion?

It is not surprising that Plutchik, in his final definition of a primary emotion, casts aside any reference to the introspective experience. "An emotion may be defined as a patterned bodily reaction of either destruction, reproduction, incorporation, orientation, protection, deprivation, rejection, or some combination of these, which is brought about by a stimulus."[17] Nothing in this definition hints of emotions as related to bodily reactions.

In short, Plutchik's ultimate resort to an observable, biologically universal criterion for primary emotions has left him with patterns of behavior that in fact can be identified with emotions only if he can trust introspection, his correlation of emotions as consciously experienced with behavior, and the normative meaning of <u>adaptive</u>. In any case, many emotional states--take one's emotional response to the cadences of a sonnet, to a symphony, a ballet, a sculpture, a painting--are hardly adaptive in any purely biological sense at least.

My concern here is by no means to deny that prototypic needs may be organismically universal. It is that, on Plutchik's view, these needs are identified as primary emotions only by a <u>tour de force</u>. And this <u>tour de force</u> is required because of the presumed need to avoid relying on introspection, in the interest of a universality that includes all the rungs of the evolutionary ladder. In the end, however, it turns out that we recognize such universal patterns as emotions because it happens--how else?--that we experience them as emotions. But in Plutchik's view, the range of primary emotions as experienced cannot speak for itself; it must fit the Procustean bed of the universal, biologically adaptive, prototypic patterns!

Before turning to Magda Arnold's analysis of the nature of emotion, it will be well to bring together considerations that seem to be conditions for me to keep in mind as I work toward a theory of primary emotions in persons.

C.   Conditions for an adequate theory
      of emotion in persons

First, however appreciative I may have been and am of
what others see, in the end I am sobered by the fact that my
actual range and depth of feelings and emotions are narrower
and shallower than I recognize. I can only hope that what
seems clearer to me, and what I build on as I proceed, will
be supported by reasonable considerations and by my reader's
own awareness and reflections.

Second, my actual experiences are never neatly captured
by my linguistic nets. Just as I must not allow myself to
be trapped by talk about the "ocean" or the "bedrock" of
feeling, so must I beware of thinking that I experience
"emotion." I shall be closer to the truth if I try to
capture the salient "moments" of my hedonic and emotive
activities. The predicament we face in capturing the
quality of hedonic and emotive experience is like that of
describing a landscape where mountains, hills, and dales
predominate, even though the landscape before our eyes is
always fuller than the dominant aspects we find ourselves
focusing on as guides to discerning subtler aspects. Here,
on the whole, nearness must yield to the larger perspective
if we are to be adequately appreciative of what is
nevertheless there, in the larger context of our experience,
as plateaus and valleys.

Third--to call attention to further complications beyond the edges of my competence--we grasp the specific poignancy of Shylock's, Lear's, or Lady Macbeth's "agony" in-and-through the language of the poet. In such successful artistic contexts, do we, perhaps, come closest to the identification of specific nuances of some feelings and emotions? Does even the moral and religious genius not communicate his profoundest emotional experience except in a language which--whether it seems to be a language of description, meditation, argument, exhortation, or lyrical reaction to experience--has in reality become the language of art? In short, in becoming sensitive to the limitations of our verbal nets for the different ranges of human experience, we need to be equally sensitive to contexts and contours within and beyond us that seem to capture, or at least point to, what words themselves alone fail to grasp.

Fourth, aware of the aspirations and frustrations of attempts to get a more solid grip on these undeniably important ingredients of our human existence, I can understand why some scholars pin their hopes for understanding our experiences of feelings and emotions on the publicly observable, physiological and behavioral patterns of persons. Nevertheless, I must now press what seems to me to be the decisive considerations against depending solely upon physiological and behavioral dynamics for understanding of emotions in persons.

I have been urging that, even assuming involvement of physiological and behavioral functioning in experiences of emotions, there should be more caution about affirming specific connections of emotive qualities with physiological and behavioral correlates. C. G. Jung's comment is to the point here. "It is extremely difficult, if not impossible, to think of a psychic function as independent of its organ, although in actual fact we experience the psychic process apart from its relation to the organic substrate. For the psychologist, however, it is the totality of these experiences that constitutes the object of investigation, and for this reason he must abjure a terminology borrowed from the anatomist."[18]

Fifth, my fundamental reason for seeking guidance in careful introspective accounts of our experiences of emotions may be condensed in one sentence. Changes from one emotional state to another do depend on the changes in the meaning of a situation to the experient. For example, if I experience an unexpected, hearty slap on the back, my total bodily state and the cortical-hypothalamic response will be involved as I experience, let us say, anger. But note: the bodily state remains relatively the same but my anger dies the moment I turn and see that an old friend is greeting me.

To generalize: even assuming that there is a cortical-hypothalamic correlate for all changes in emotions, such physiological changes do not give me the clue to the particular change, say, from my anger to my delight as the meaning of my old friend's slap replaces the initial meaning. Again, could we pin-point physiological changes as correlations to emotive changes more accurately than we actually can, would they _alone_ help us understand the particular qualities of remorse experienced, say, by Judas who betrayed Jesus and by Peter who denied him? Or do we have ground here for taking seriously the view that the person's psyche operates _also_ in accordance with patterns of change that will evade us if they are not examined in their own right?

Magda Arnold, in commenting on the James-Lange theory, that our emotions follow the visceral changes and behavior ("I am sorry because I cry"), makes the definitive point against any theories that would seek to distinguish the quality of the emotional state entirely by reference to bodily changes, inner or overt. "But surely there is a decided difference between the joy that comes from wine and the joy of the lover when he meets his beloved, a difference that cannot be explained by pointing to the abstract knowledge of a difference in cause. The lover now has what he loves and wants and is glad."[19]

Sixth, these comments, I pause to note, would of themselves favor the unity and complexity of the total person presented on other grounds (chapters One through Three). Granted that we never neglect the best contextual description in consciousness, we cannot be assured of a more complete view and theory of a particular emotion if we do not observe and theorize as to the way in which it is related to the lived-body, the unconscious, and the conceptual Body. Prima facie, emotions have their own quality and dynamic as experienced, but this does not mean that their very appearance leaves other questions about them unanswered. We cannot, to be sure, anticipate by some general theory of mind what factors go into the appearance, into the dynamics, and into the "life-history" of any specific emotion. But the view to be advanced allows for beginning with an introspective account and enlarging it, as need requires, by noting its relation to the lived-body and to the conceptual Body. Some emotions as experienced may bear no witness to the conceptual Bodily events (or the metaphysical events); and, once we "save the appearances" (Plato), we can proceed without being inhibited by the fact that the supposedly more explanatory physiological -behavioral factors elude us so far.

D.   Magda Arnold's theory of emotion

1. A person experiences an emotion; and something is the occasion for that experience. In emotion, as in perception, there is a subject and a reference to an object. The object need not, of course, be outside the person; it may be

present, remembered, anticipated, or merely imagined. To be
the object of an emotion, however, the object must become
part of a larger framework or field. For Magda Arnold it
must be appraised "as desirable or undesirable, valuable or
harmful for me, so that I am drawn toward it or repelled by
it."[20]

This tenet is repeated over and over again. "To arouse
an emotion, the object must be appraised as affecting me in
some way, affecting me personally as an individual with my
particular experience and my particular aims."[21] No
experient, no emotion; for the emotion reflects an appraisal
of the object.

2. But can it be that the appraisal itself is the emotion?
If a person loves another, does his loving consist merely in
estimating him to be good for him? Surely not, for one can
know that another is the person who is good for him and yet
feel no attraction. "Emotion seems to include not only the
appraisal of how this thing or person will affect me but
also a definite pull toward or away from it. In fact, does
not the emotional quale consist precisely in that
unreasoning involuntary attraction or repulsion?...But if I
think something is good for me here and now, and feel myself
drawn toward it, sometimes even against my better judgment,
then my experience is, properly speaking, nonrational;...it
is an addition to knowledge; it is emotional."[22]

For Arnold, then, something more than rational approval

-or-disapproval of the object's relation to me is the condition of emotion. The _emotional_ _quale_ will not occur if I do not "feel myself drawn," or "pulled toward or away from," the object as perceived. The context makes clear that for Arnold the words "nonrational" and "unreasoning" are not synonyms for "against my better judgment." "Nonrational" and "unreasoning" refer only to the contention that emotion is not an inference, just as the experience of the color "red" is not the product of any inferential process. Thus, to say that one experiences anger or jealousy "against my better judgment" is to say that one does not approve of these nonrational emotive states as responses to a situation.

I stress this point because emotions are frequently, in everyday speech and in more theoretical discussion, spoken of as being "unreasonable," or contra-reason. The fact is that a person may be gripped by a (nonrational) emotion without being unreasonable. In underscoring the impact upon the person of an emotional response as something "brute"-- as itself a nonrational _quale_ added to the situation as appraised--Arnold is emphasizing that reason-capable persons contend with total situations within which there are nonreasoned emotional attractions or repulsions.

Let us imagine parents who might find themselves, after the explosion of a hydrogen bomb, safe in their shelter. But one of their three children, a son, is too far away, at the time of the explosion, to reach the shelter. They soon see him approaching the shelter, but they know that he has been exposed to radiation, and that if he is allowed to enter the shelter they too will be vulnerable. Let us say that their emotional response to his situation is so strong that they explore every possiblility of protecting him. Their reasoning does not come, emotion-free, into "an emotional situation." They are experiencing both thinking and emotions as they now try to decide what will be best. They know that, if they open the shelter to this son, the other two children as well as they themselves will be exposed to radiation. Yet the pull of that son's plight may issue in their "casting aside" reasonableness. Whatever they do involves, as we say, "mixed emotions." Their decision to help him involves suppressing the emotive pulls favorable to protecting the children who will be endangered by allowing him into the shelter. If one decides that their action was unreasonable, it means not that "reason was overcome by emotion" but that one complex of emotions rather than another was deemed the more reasonable, emotional way out.

I am not suggesting, of course, that feeling-emotive states necessarily make the achievement of reasonable goals easier or harder. I am suggesting that a person intent on "becoming reasonable" is involved in experiential situations with such nonrational factors as sense, feelings, and emotions that are not in their essence anti-reasonable. Hence, a person is not "first" a complex of sensory, affective, and emotive components with which his reason has "then" to "contend." No figures of speech about reason --say as a pilot or charioteer challenged and threatened by these nonrational factors--should seduce us into thinking that the person's reason is somehow always working against nonrational odds. The "world" a person lives by is what he, as a knower, evaluator, and actor, can make of the nonrational factors in his experience as he interacts with his ambient.

3. I have emphasized that, for Arnold, while there can not be an emotion without the nonrational pull toward or away from, neither can there be an emotion without appraisal of the relation between the person and object--in terms of "good for" or "bad for," harmful or not harmful, favorable or not favorable. Because this particular interpretation of the evaluative relation--already present in her theory of "pleasant" and "unpleasant"--is a point of critical disagreement, let us examine the text carefully. There is no doubt that the emotional response presupposes an appraisal that is direct, immediate, or intuitive. "The appraisal that arouses an emotion is not abstract; it is not the result of reflection. It is immediate and indeliberate. If we see somebody stab at our eye with his finger, we avoid the threat instantly, even though we may know that he does

not intend to hurt or even to touch us. <u>Before we can make
such an instant response, we have estimated somehow that the
stabbing finger could hurt</u>. Since the movement is
immediate, unwitting, or even contrary to our better
knowledge, this <u>appraisal</u> of possible harm must be similarly
immediate."[23]

Arnold at this point also refers to the fact that
children and animals seem to know what is harmful or not as
the basis for further learning. "They may have to learn, of
course, that some judgments are mistaken."[24] She adds:
"There must be a psychological capacity of appraising how a
given thing will affect us, whether it will hurt or please
us, before we want to approach or avoid it. To call upon
mere `learning,' `past experience,' or the `conditioned
reflex' for an explanation is futile. Without such an
appraisal, learning would be impossible and past experience
useless."[25] For example, we could not "condition" the fear
-response were it not an unlearned response supplying the
base for extending fear to new objects or situations.
Without such a prereflective <u>given</u> there would be no
emotion. It is "meaning" at this pre-analytic level that is
central to the very being of any emotion. Even when the
intuitive appraisal becomes more reflective, "the emotion
changes with the new intuitive estimate which follows the
corrective judgment," but "whenever there is no intuitive

appraisal...but only a reflective judgment...there is no emotion."[26]

4. So much is at stake for our theory of emotion that I shall here pay special attention to what Arnold impressively articulates as her view, under her sub-topic, "Perception completed by appraisal."[27] On Arnold's view, for a person to perceive that what is approaching is a ball requires the integration of visual sense impressions with those from other modalities. But to know that the approaching ball is a threat calls for an additional act of primary appraisal, equally primary and unreflective as sense-knowing, which estimates the ball as harmful or good. I quote several instructive passages: "The process by which we estimate whether a thing is harmful or good for us is similarly direct and intuitive, hidden from inspection. A fear or anger reaction follows so quickly upon a sudden threat that it may be all but impossible to separate perception, appraisal, and emotion."[28] "Thus, following upon perception and completing it, appraisal makes possible an active approach, acceptance or withdrawal, and thus establishes our relation to the world."[29] Again: "The intuitive appraisal of the situation initiates an action tendency that is felt as emotion, expressed in various bodily changes, and that eventually may lead to overt action."[30]

In this last sentence something has been added that seems ambiguous. The emotion is not the action tendency but is the action tendency as felt. That ambiguous word "felt" is not helpful here, for it may mean that the action tendency, of which the percipient is aware, is the emotion. Or it may mean that the emotion is the conscious accompaniment of the action tendency already initiated by intuitive appraisal. This relation of tendency to emotion is not an unimportant issue in the debate about the nature of primary emotion especially, as we shall see.

Arnold's intent to distinguish between emotion and perception is clear, but whether the emotion is the action tendency or the consciusness of it remains in doubt. I take it that Arnold's intention to distinguish between perception and action-emotion is evident in the following quotation, but it leaves me unsure about the exact relation of appraisal, perception, emotion, and behavior. "...the same perception results sometimes in one and sometimes in another emotion and action... First I see something [perception], then I realize that it is dangerous [appraisal] --and as soon as I do, I am afraid [emotion] and run [behavior]. Since this appraisal is almost [!] as direct as sense perception and immediately follows and completes it, it can be known as a separate process only when we come to reflect upon it."31

It would seem that emotion completes the perceptual process. Does it? Or is there a total perceptual Gestalt of which the emotive tendency is an intrinsic part? As I shall contend, Arnold's reflections lead me to pose the underlying questions: (a) How is the emotion connected with the action tendency resulting from the appraisal? (b) Is the emotion the awareness of the tendency that results from the appraisal? Or is the emotion a conscious accompaniment intimately connected with the tendency?

In Arnold's summary-definition, tendency is as essential as appraisal, and the physiological-behavioral patterns express the appraisal and tendency. In her words, emotion is "the felt tendency toward anything intuitively appraised as good (beneficial), or away from anything intuitively appraised as bad (harmful). This attraction or aversion is accompanied by a pattern of physiological changes organized toward approach or withdrawal. The patterns differ for different emotions."[32]

In a more recent pronouncement, she says: "The emotion becomes [!] a felt tendency toward anything appraised as good, and away from anything appraised as bad. This definition allows us to specify how emotion is related to action: if nothing interferes, the felt tendency will lead to action... And as we appraise the situation as more desirable or more harmful, we become aware not only that we tend toward or away from it, but also that this is an emotional tendency."[33]

E.   Evaluation of Arnold's theory of emotion

Arnold's account cannot but command respect. It is based on page after page of critical reviews of studies that concern themselves with many aspects of emotion in animal, child, adolescent, and adult; it seeks to harmonize physiological, behavioral, and phenomenological observations; the systematic concern is extremely helpful in clarifying issues.

1. To put my basic difficulty directly: Can we encompass the range of emotions under the appraisals "beneficial or harmful?" I am extending the comment already made regarding the difficulty that arises from accounting for the variety of hedonic tones under the broad appraisals "impeding or unimpeding of a function." Judgments of "harmful" and "beneficial" cannot do justice to the variety of emotions. Can we say that the emotion "tenderness" is beneficial in the same way as the emotion "wonder" is? Are "lust," "anger," "elation," capable of being classified as beneficial or harmful without qualification?

Furthermore, do we somehow know that a given object would be harmful in a way, say, that arouses anger as opposed to fear, or beneficial in a way, say, that arouses tenderness, or sympathy, or lust, or wonder? Allowing for later correction of intuitive appraisals, one still is left asking: Why does this particular emotion, rather than that, express the kind of harm or good confronted? However, as I have already asked, does the percipient have a built-in norm for harmful and beneficial?

The question: How do we know what is good and bad? is a large one. Here, in accordance with what I have earlier argued about not packing "survival" with qualitative value, I suggest that, rather than themselves presupposing some appraisal of beneficial or harmful, the emotions, with their hedonic tones, are themselves involved in our seeking a criterion of beneficial and harmful. We cannot at this point say that certain emotions are a means to some goal called goodness (or to avoidance of evil). Even restricting myself to what I shall call "primary emotions," I suggest that "our emotions" are "raw" data that will themselves be involved in our defining the good. Granted that every emotion is a response involving some meaning, that meaning does not carry with it, or presuppose, what would have to remain a very inclusive definition of "beneficial and harmful."

2. There is an underlying presupposition in Arnold's thinking that is not uncommon in interpretations of feelings and emotion. I grant that to be alive is to be purposive, and this of course includes "survival." Moreover, this purposive thrust is readily laden not only with a conceptual crutch that we refer to as the "will to live" but also with a hidden conception of "harmful" or "beneficial" (that may

even extend to: "to be alive" is as such "the good"). So I press here: the will to live is an abstraction that cannot be given specific normative meaning in terms of the inner activity-demands that are concrete "directions" (the tend -encies). If we bear this in mind, we shall not say that the will to live is some independent inner striving--I almost said an homunculus--in terms of which appraisals are made as the basis for feelings and emotions.

3. What may here be operating is what I would call the fallacy of evolutionary thinking about man--if this did not suggest disparagement of biological evolution. But, as I hope my contexts have made clear, one commits this fallacy when he thinks of man's feelings, emotions, and reason as additives to the stream and current of "evolution" in which the will to survive is the common factor. Yet, I must persist, there is no will to live definable apart from what it means for a particular kind of being, given the quality of his being, to remain alive as that qualitative being. For the amoeba to live is for the amoeba to feel its level of hedonic tone; feeling (pleasant or unpleasant) is not an addendum to its "staying alive." For the dog to live is for the dog to be alive as a being capable of its level of sensing, perceiving, feeling, and emoting... The dog does not, any more than the amoeba, have the will to live and then sense, perceive, feel, and emote in order to improve its chances of living. Amoeba, dog, or man, a survivor is

always a particular kind of being, defined by its dimensions of activity-potential. Persons are not animals who survive the better "because" frontal lobes are added to their cortex. A person is a new being, a being whose life and growth and death, comprise a novel meaning for both "existence" and "survival." We may now include, among his constitutive activity-potentials, feelings and emotions that are uniquely personal even if some of them resemble those of subpersonal beings. In any case, we may not establish an ethics on some abstraction called "survival," or on a "pleasure principle," or on a theory of emotions (primary or not) as such.

F.   Reflective overview

Emotions, as Arnold emphasizes, bring their own ranges of quality into the experience of persons. They are themselves catalysts of different changes in experience and behavior. Yet, if I am correct, Arnold, in thinking of feelings and emotions as favorable or unfavorable to the more elemental struggle for survival, seems to end up with an instrumental view of emotions. My protest is that the qualities of the emotive experiences themselves need to enter into the meaning of survival for persons, for the terms "beneficial" and "harmful" require a norm for survival that is not provided. In the theory I shall advance the emphasis will be on distinguishing certain emotive qualities, _ab_ _initio_ with their own characteristic _tend_-encies for change that enter into the person's learning what is best for him (in ways that involve whatever reflection he is capable of at different stages of development). The emotive knowing -willing person, forever active as a unique, complex matrix of being-becoming, is no neutral _tabula_ _rasa_. His responses are not merely reactions to an ambient. His emotive (nonrational) activities (ever interacting with the Environment) enter into the very meaning of what quality his survival can come to realize, but they do not presuppose a norm for the survival of the person.

In the following chapters I shall try to distinguish what I shall call _primary_ _emotive_ _tendencies_ (or primary emotions) at the pre-analytic level of personal existence. I am aware that this calls for deciding, from amongst the myriad emotive states with their varying complexity, which emotions are unlearned. This problem is so beset with difficulties that my reader might well suppose that only one ignorant of the history of reflection on this type of question would dare to introduce it. But can we remain satisfied with the claim that "human beings are basically emotional" without trying to determine what the actual (at least minimal) range of different unlearned emotive tendencies is at the level of persons?

We do experience emotions. Provided we do not think of distinctions as separations, we can, I believe, make some progress. Our problem is more difficult than, yet not different from, the psychological search for elemental colors (red, green, for example) as opposed to blends and fusions (like orange). We cannot avoid such problems as: Are all of our emotions learned? Accordingly, our search for primary emotions is the search for species-wide, irreducible, unlearned activity-potentials as experienced by the being-becoming person. Obviously, in order for an activity-potential to be irreducible or unlearned does not require that it be present, fully developed, at birth. Nobody claims that all cognitive activity-potentials are fully developed at birth, or that they are all learned. Be all this as it may, the task before me is the more formidable because I believe that primary emotions are identical with primary motives.

Notes for Chapter Five

1. William James, The *Varieties* *of* *Religious* *Experience*
    (London: Longmans, Green, 1905), 150.

2. Charles Winkelmans de Cléty, *The* *World* *of* *Persons*
    (London: Burns and Oates, 1967), 142.

3. Karl H. Pribham, "Feelings as Monitors" in *Feelings* *and*
    Emotions, ed. Magda Arnold (New York: Academic Press,
    1970), 44, and see 52.

4. Karl H. Pribham, ibid., 52. Similar comments would
    apply to K. T. Strongman's behavioral account of emotion
    in his *The* *Psychology* *of* *Emotion* (New York: Wiley,
    1973), see 87, 90, 193ff.

5. R. S. Peters, "Emotions and the Category of Passivity"
    in *Proceedings* *of* *the* *Aristotelian* *Society*, 1961-62:
    117-134. On this theme, see V. J. McGill, ibid., 53f.,
    and R. W. Leeper, "A Motivational Theory of Emotions to
    Replace `Emotions as a Disorganized Response' in
    Psychol. *Rev.* 55 (1948): 5-21.

6. Robert Plutchik, *The* *Emotions*: *Facts*, *Theories*, *and* *a*
    New *Model* (New York: Random House, 1962), 20. The
    underlying theory of emotion I am criticizing here
    reappears with a significant expansion in Plutchik's
    Emotion, *A* *Psycho-Evolutionary* *Synthesis* (New York:
    Harper and Row, 1980).

7. John T. MacCurdy, The Psychology of Emotion (Morbid and Normal) (London: Kegan Paul, 1925), 41.

8. Robert Plutchik, ibid., 45.

9. Ibid., 55.

10. Ibid.

11. Ibid., 56.

12. Ibid., 63.

13. Ibid.

14. Ibid., 8, 9.

15. Ibid., 71.

16. Ibid.

17. Ibid., 151.

18. Carl G. Jung, "The Spirit of Psychology," in vol. 1, Spirit and Nature: Papers from the Eranos Yearbooks (New York and London, 1957): 388, italics added.

19. Magda Arnold, vol. 1. Emotion and Personality (New York: Columbia University Press, 1960), 111.

20. Ibid., 171.

21. Ibid.

22. Ibid., 172.

23. Ibid., italics added.

24. Ibid.

25. Ibid., 173.

26. Ibid., 175, 176.

27. Ibid., 176.

28. Ibid., 177.

29. Ibid., 176.

30. Ibid., 177.

31. Ibid., 178.

32. Ibid., 182.

33. Magda Arnold, ed. <u>Feelings and Emotions</u> (New York: Academic Press, 1970), 176. Arnold's chapter, "Perennial Problems in the Field of Emotion," is an excellent review of issues and of her own response to them.

CHAPTER SIX

Can Primary Emotions Be Primary Motives?

A.   Persistent issues and some conclusions

Several conclusions, emerging from our study of human
emotion so far, are part of my defense for offering the far
from obvious theory that primary emotions and primary
motives are identical as constitutive strivings in persons.
It will be well to set out briefly some of these conclusions
as background for further discussion.

1. Any account of human emotions must not be led astray by
using emotional states in animals (or presumable
physiological or behavioral analogues) as trustworthy
prototypes for human emotions. When a psychologist, hoping
to avoid difficulties in introspective analysis, relies for
his theory of emotion on such analogies, he is trying to
cash checks for money he did not have in the bank to begin
with. That is, he is trying to link behavior with emotions

that, presumably, he cannot inspect with any confidence in his own experience.

2. We cannot allow biological and behavioral norms of health alone to be foundations for our distinguishing human emotions in all their variety. For some criterion of "strength" and "weakness" in response, of "organizing" and "disorganizing" modes of adaptation, is invariably assumed, with biological survival of some quality usually intended. For the person, the issue that is central is the quality of survival--that cannot be reduced to sheer continuance of existence.

3. To put my dominant concern positively, an adequate theory of human emotions will be guided by the inspection of them as they are experienced in the complex of personal consciousness (including their relations to organic and behavioral contents, as called for). If we are guided by the personal context as a whole, I doubt that we shall hear claims that, because some emotions are sometimes "upsetting" or "obscuring," they belong to an earlier stage of evolution, or to atavistic obstructions issuing from the oldest part of the brain.

4. However, as I seek a more adequate view, I must admit at the outset that I have been constantly haunted by the difficulties of trying to distinguish primary emotions in the first place and then of trying to differentiate them from what are so easily called "complex" or "compound"

emotions--as if a psychological physics or chemistry were possible! The spectrum of what we call (so roughly!) the "affective" and the "emotional" life is so broad, the "movement" from one moment of hedonic and emotive tone to another so hard to follow, that one always wonders whether he has distinguished only to destroy the Gestalten in experience. Why not simply admit that the so-called stream of conscious experience still winds its way so mysteriously in the complexities of our being that our attempts to capture them will inevitably lead us into theoretical and conceptual thickets?

Why indeed re-open questions that seem no longer to disturb scholars who are all but disdainful of lists of innate needs and emotions? Thus, Professor Harold B. Gerard says: "Lists of this sort [unlearned motives] went out of fashion a long time ago for good reason. Following McDougall, writers with lists typically present them as though the items in the list really exist and somewhere in the person there is a set of valves that can be turned on individually or in combinations. Labelling drive states [or primary emotions, as I shall call them] can be an absorbing past time, and such lists can get very long with some containing as many as 25 pseudo-distinct drives or instincts."[1] Were this a description of the actual situation rather than a high-handed and incorrect rendering of what psychologists like McDougall actually claim, were the analogy of a set of valves not the very one which instinct-theorists like McDougall reject, one might indeed be stopped in his tracks. Nevertheless, this passage describes an attitude that prides itself on being more empirical and more scholarly--and, alas, "fashionable!"

Support for this kind of attack is ample in Warren Shibles' book, Emotion.[2] Yet Shibles' book convinces me more than ever that the theory of emotion is witness to philosophical orientations that are not explicit. For example, Shibles seems neither to see the consequences of the extreme nominalism he advocates, nor that he himself is substituting for the reification of "emotions" the reification of "language." He says, for example, that there is no such thing as "fear," but that this is a word, dictated by linguistic custom, to designate behavioral activities. If this is the case, in view of the fact that there are many, many behavioral acts referred to by "fear," how does one decide which of these acts are the "paradigmatic" acts that qualify them as "fear." And, indeed, how does one decide what acts are to be called "fear" and what acts "anger"?

Furthermore, Shibles, seeking refuge in a "lingo-centric predicament," can say that "taking language as our epistemological starting point ... the "I" in "I speak" has meaning only in language..."[3] But if "emotion" is nothing by itself, why is "language?" Indeed, are there meanings of words that exist independently of speakers? To this Shibles no doubt has a reply in the words "one can have language without thought but one cannot have thought without language."[4] My basic concern still remains: What is the justification for a particular criterion of word-usage, for referents of words such as "physiological" or "psychological balance?" To what does a word like "state" refer unless one can specify what it is a state of? The scholar who avoids the risk of labelling does not avoid the greater risk of unintelligibility.

5. An instance of the situation that our concern for accuracy, within the context of adequacy to the conscious experience of persons, may now be suggested. Let the reader imagine looking at a ballet (accompanied by music). Setting aside the problems of the aesthetic evaluation, let him try to keep track of the stream of feelings and emotions that he experiences as he follows the music and the movement of the dance. Who can possibly find the words to describe "the flow of stress"--even if he could clearly distinguish one movement from its crescendo to diminuendo, or articulate the shift from one qualitative experience to another? Or let the reader imagine himself responding to a play like Hamlet where conceptual meanings are more accessible. Once more, the hedonic and emotional experiences have a way of gripping the participant and taking him on a journey that defies linguistic description. Responding, he exclaims: "How

powerful!" But what does the exclamation mean precisely? Yet our difficulty in answering does not hide unique responses to the rhythm and pattern that Shakespeare worked into his tragedy.

It seems plain, as we reflect on such experiences, that the "stream" or "torrent" of our hedonic and emotive experiencing is not made up of "emotions" or "drives," and that the "hills" and "slopes" and "valleys" in our emotional panorama do have a "total" quality which does indeed keep changing and escaping our verbal nets. No wonder we are inclined to give up and talk about "the emotions," and use the word "emotional" to refer to--so far as I can make out-- responsive experiences that simply overflow any verbal expression. Granted also that we properly fret lest to distinguish is to separate. Nor can we forget--as in responding to a ballet, or to Hamlet--that we experience many more feelings and emotions than we can designate by any word.

On the other hand, we do not remain mute, and we do proceed to talk about anger, fear, lust, elation, sympathy, respect--and about more complex emotive responses. And we do believe that our labels, inadequate as they are, will not inevitably miss the total qualitative experiences and their changes. Again, reference to hills, slopes, and valleys in our perceptual experiences may be instructive--just as we do talk about the colors of the panorama, even though we are aware of the difficulties in expressing perceptual variations and the "in-between" colors. We prefer, with good reason, not to speak _only_ of sensory-perceptual states; and we have searched for primary colors and their correlates and conditions.

6. In sum, my underlying thesis is that it will no longer do to talk about "emotional states" without realizing that the states are distinguishable within the ranges of qualities of emotive experiences. The hazards of "lists" and "reification" are not as great as the dangers of referring to "feelings" and "emotions" and "drives" to account for experiences of "excitement," without attending to the distinctions between them by which we are actually living. I proceed, then, following the footsteps of others, chastened by a sense of the dangers both of analysis and synthesis, but unwilling to deceive myself into thinking that "objective correlations" can be adequately established without such self-awareness as we are capable of distinguishing more dependably. It may be that more paths are discernible in the rich context of our experience than were at first apparent. In due course I shall indicate why I think a particular emotion is primary, but I am not claiming that those I try to articulate are the only primary emotions. They are the ones I would stand by without arguing that all the other emotions are "compounded" from them.

B.   Why separate primary motives
      from primary emotions?

1. My next step is to present the groundwork for proposing
that inspection of certain emotive experiences provides the
inner clue to innate human motives. This will include
discussing issues involved in the debate about innate
motives in persons.

I shall use the term "primary motive" without further
notice as a substitute for a family of terms, insofar as
these are intended to denote unlearned purposive (telic)
dispositions: instinct, urge, instinctoid need, desire,
want, wish, propensity, drive. What is essentially in mind
are demands made by the psycho-physiological person
regardless of the specific environment, physical and social,
in which he learns, in various ways, to gratify these
demands.

2. Twentieth century thinking about primary motives has
understandably been influenced by controversies about man's
place in biological evolution. Whether we are thinking of
psychologists, anthropologists, sociologists, theologians,
or philosophers, the underlying issue concerns two
requirements, that for accuracy and that for adequacy.

The priority of (objective) accuracy led to a merciless
pruning of the conflicting lists of primary motives that
stopped only with those whose universality could be defended

by pointing at least to species-wide physiological processes. This pruning encouraged, and was encouraged by, the concern lest human conduct, good or bad, be attributed to unlearned attributes of man when in fact there is a likelihood that human behavior, thinking, and valuing are the product of learning in social and natural environments.

Some consequences of this pruning will be noted concretely as counter-proposals are made. What deserves attention now is the curious fact that even the primary motives that did survive such pruning were often referred to as emotions--fear and anger, for example. It was hardly "loose nomenclature" alone that resulted in all but interchangeable appeal to both emotions and instincts as fundamental, constitutional forces in human nature. In any case, there remains a widespread situation in which emotions are saluted as motivating factors in the development of personality, although they are left dangling, or neglected, even in explicit systems of motivation.

For example, so sensitive and systematic a psychologist of personality as Gordon W. Allport could write a monumental work like Personality: A Psychological Interpretation (1937) without even one page on emotion. The thorough revision of that book, Pattern and Growth in Personality (1961), included one page on emotion. Yet crucial to the theory of personality in both versions was a critique of instinct theory and a substitute theory of motivation. Nor does scrutiny of Abraham Maslow's influential Motivation and Personality (1954), nor of Karl Jaspers' compendium, General Psychopathology (1963) yield better results.

One wonders whether exasperation combined with diffidence when William James commented: "The merely descriptive literature of the emotions is one of most tedious parts of psychology...I should as lief read verbal descriptions of the shapes of the rocks on a New Hampshire farm. They give nowhere a central point of view or a deductive or generative principle."[6] Notwithstanding, the same James begins his chapter "Emotions," which follows that on instincts, with the words: "In speaking of the instincts it has been impossible to keep them separate from the emotional excitements which go with them....Every object that excites an instinct excites an emotion as well."[7]

Much more could be added to illustrate the two-mindedness that characterizes so much work on emotions and primary motives. Many agree that both motives and emotions are sources of change in the person experiencing them. But it is hard to account for the all but separate treatment of each as sources of power, structure, and of development in persons. In this situation, I have long sought a theory of primary motivation that would express the actual unity consciously experienced when we undergo some of our emotions as motives. I found A. F. Shand speaking to my experience when he said: "...ask yourself whither they are tending. For the emotions have complex tendencies. They have their own impulses, even the most quiescent. By their ends you may know them...define them by their ends."[8]

For years it has seemed to me that William McDougall, that highly independent, fertile, and systematic psychologist, took the right line as he related (primary) emotions and innate motives. So I shall focus on presenting the view that commanded much attention in the first decades of the twentieth century, a view of motivation that concerned itself not only with universal (primary) motives and emotions but also with the way in which they were responsive to environmental influences.

C.   The nature of instincts on McDougall's view

In 1923, in Outline of Psychology, McDougall defines an instinct as follows: "an innate disposition which determines the organism to perceive (to pay attention to) any object of a certain class and to experience in its presence a certain emotional excitement and an impulse to action which find expression in a specific mode of behavior in relation to that object."[9]

Such has been the controversy that has raged over this definition that a preliminary comment will at least help to dispel misunderstandings that are hardly justified by McDougall's text.

First, _disposition_. In a footnote on the same page McDougall makes clear his own preference for thinking of a disposition as psycho-physiological, "because it clearly implies that the disposition plays a part in determining both bodily action and the course of experience."[10]

Second, _innate_. McDougall does not restrict the word "innate" to mean present at birth. With the facts of maturation in mind, he is simply saying that, whenever they do mature, these psycho-physiological dispositions are themselves directive factors in the actual learning that takes place. Perception in good part is what it is because unlearned and learned dispositions render the agent sensitive to some "stimuli" more than to others. The whole problem of unlearned perception might well stir controversy, and we shall turn to it in a moment.

Third, McDougall is using the term "object" in "the very widest sense, namely to include not only material things and organisms, but also various situations in which the creature may find itself, consisting in conjunctions of internal and external conditions."[11] Object is not a thing, necessarily, but whatever the disposition selectively responds to. (In similar contexts, I shall use the compound word "object -objective" to emphasize that the "object" must be seen psychologically as evoking the dispositional _tend_-ency.)

Fourth, specific mode of behavior. It is hard to see why some readers assumed that McDougall's view favored unlearned, rigid modes of response--a view that would defy, especially, human differences in modes of response. But closer attention to full context could not miss McDougall's emphasis that the higher the species in the evolutionary scale, its action pattern is neither rigid, nor rigidly geared to one object (or to "class" of objects). Rather does it involve "variation of movements, adapting them to special circumstances in such a way as to make for the attainment of a goal."[12] Surely such passages do not lend themselves to F. V. Smith's interpretation. "In McDougall's system an innate neural organization is held to prescribe the form of perception or the significance which a given situation may have for the organism."[13] For McDougall holds neither to an exclusively neural innate organization, nor to a psycho-physiological organism fitted out with a panoply of particular responses to be triggered off by a "given situation." And McDougall specifically states that the "object" is any object of certain class, that behavior can vary in accordance with the meaning given the object within that class, and that one should expect more variation in human than in other creatures.

For McDougall, in sum, the human mind is no tabula rasa. The evolutionary changes we trace, and those we note in each person, cannot be understood without reference to motivating dispositions intrinsic to each kind or level of creature in evolutionary development. And the particular object -objective within the class, definable by the purposive tendency of the motive, will be affected by the cognitive capacity of the individual (in the context of his past learning). All the more must we examine the place of emotion in this total process.

D.   McDougall's view of the relation
       of emotion to instinct

Three initial statements will introduce us to McDougall's view of primary emotions. First, in Outline of Psychology (1923), he states that primary emotions are "essentially indicators of the working of instinctive impulses."[14] That is, primary emotions are not the instinctive impulses, but effects of them in consciousness. Furthermore, like the instinctive impulses, "they signify to us primarily not the nature of things, but rather the nature of our impulsive reactions to things."[15]

Second, it is somewhat surprising to me that McDougall's criterion for a primary emotion is strongly influenced by evidence of "a similar emotion and impulse...clearly displayed in the instinctive activities of the higher animals."[16] Another factor in McDougall's interpretation of the relation of emotion to instinct is the presence of "the emotion and impulse," in exaggerated, morbid intensity, in human beings. He interprets such data to mean that the instincts are relatively independent, functional units in the mental constitution. Thus, comparative psychology and mental pathology play guiding and confirmatory roles in McDougall's choice of primary emotions.

But, third, what is especially puzzling to me is the pains that McDougall takes to distinguish the conative from the emotional process. He writes explicitly: "The propriety of distinguishing between the conative element in consciousness, the impulse, appetite, desire, or aversion, and the accompanying emotion is not so obvious. For these features are most intimately and constantly associated, and introspective discrimination is usually difficult."[17]

It is this "associated" relation of the emotion to the conative tendency that I am particularly calling in question. To begin with, the relation of "accompaniment" is not given in any emotion as experienced. Moreover, how can we be guided by the "evidence" of emotions in the higher animals if our own immediate data are not adequately distinguished and interpreted? McDougall, or any other observer, may well be guided by similarities in physiological development, and he may find more than hints, as we have noted Plutchik does in the adaptive or non-adaptive behavior in animals.

But we simply go too far beyond our evidence if such procedure permits us to restrict the number of human primary emotions, and of primary motives, to the physiological tendencies that man "shares" with the higher animals. This procedure seems to influence strongly McDougall's conclusion that primary emotions are accompaniments of conative tendencies. Yet, does it help us to know what it means experientially to say that a primary emotion accompanies a conative disposition? McDougall seems to be holding that a primary emotion is at once to be an accompaniment of and an efflorescent factor within the conative disposition. James Drever, McDougall's careful student and creative follower, in saying that emotions can disturb the expected flow of intellectual and behavioral functions, seems clearly to grant a certain impulsive autonomy to emotions themselves-- even as McDougall seems at times to suggest.[18]

The view I shall propose moves further in the direction of granting autonomy to emotions as experienced, whatever the relation to organic changes may or may not be. Explicitly, the emotions are themselves, as consciously experienced, the impulsive striving (tendency) toward certain goals. Each emotive disposition has its own hedonic tone, and is not as such a form of "feeling." But as we noted earlier (chapter Four), the total personal context influences hedonic qualities, and I am inclined to hold that there may be other inferred (unconscious) conative states that are not emotions. But the primary emotions I shall attempt to distinguish are in essence conative thrusts or tendencies as experienced. In this view, what will continue to surface is the manner in which each primary emotive response is to be understood in relation to the object -objective.

Pausing to review for a moment, Magda Arnold, we saw, postulated estimative and appraising functions as the basis for emotional experience. I protested not so much the postulating of hidden estimative functions, as our ability to use the appraisals, "beneficial" or "harmful," for determining what emotion would occur. For McDougall, emotion does not depend on estimative function. As the accompaniments of the instinctive impulse, primary emotions seem to play a part in the total conative-cognitive response that defines a particular unlearned disposition. For McDougall, emotion is involved not in the beneficial or harmful estimation in Arnold's sense, but in the innate disposition's directive thrust toward "an object of a certain class" that is being attended to, or perceived. What both views--differences in detail aside--force to surface is the underlying issue in any theory of innate motivation and primary emotion. Can a reasonable case be made for any disposition as involving unlearned (innate) tendency and meaning?

E.   The theoretical need for dispositions

1. Even casual observers of animals and persons will be impressed by their differential responses to the environment. Some "objects"--sounds, smells, tactual and visual experiences--rivet attention and evoke responses while others do not. There is no telling before the activity takes place which object will produce what response. This simple statement may be surprising. For we unthinkingly assume that our sensory experiences or our psychic and bodily states are responsive to the environment on its own terms alone, or that the stimulus, as such, triggers our response.

2. "Natural selection," we remind ourselves, indicates no conscious "selective process" on the part of Nature but only that the demands of the psycho-physiological being itself are challenged, frustrated, or supported by the pertinent environment. If we are, now more specifically, to avoid the vacuous generality of an innate disposition called the "will to live," we must face the obstinate fact that the individual organism itself seems to "select" some aspects, areas, stimuli, and not others. What seems probable, therefore, is that within the agent-person there are telic dispositions whose patterns of response are (within limits, as the case may be) modifiable. These dispositions render the person more sensitive to some objects and not others. If, for example, we discover ourselves (or observe other

beings) becoming ready to flee from some object, why should we not, with McDougall, assume some disposition inclusive of a discriminatory act--to be carefully circumscribed for each disposition?

Again, as persons we do not simply "gawk" indifferently at the world. Whatever is "out there" becomes "our world" because we find ourselves paying attention to and being incited to act in special ways to some objects and situations and not others. That is, while learning does enter into later developments, we begin not with tabula rasa natures but with initial impulsive dispositions that, in being aroused, enable us to discriminate aspects of the "field" available to our abilities that would otherwise go unnoticed. In brief, we need the concept of disposition, especially in persons, in order to explain persons' differential responses as they distinguish and build "their world" (environment) within "the World" (Environment). This general thesis needs further defense.

3. We may first note that we all grant we have dispositions based on learned experience. For example, as we pay more attention to certain objects--say a shriek rather than a laugh occurring at the same time--we plainly are experiencing selectively, or "preferring," some objects to others. We do not hesitate to postulate in such instances the development in the person of some "structure" that has

produced in him the condition of preferring what he was relatively indifferent to earlier. Whether we speak of acquired habits, or attitudes, or traits, we are talking of predisposing patterns of response involving perception (at least). These dispositions are selectively responsive without our having consciously to call them into action. Indeed, they characterize us; and it is in terms of such relatively stable, prepotent-response-Gestalten that we come to know much about what we can expect of ourselves in different situations.

While this does not establish the contention that we may infer entities or powers not consciously experienced, we are in this area not at odds with the physicist who attributes mass and energy to a body, not because he observes them, but because he needs to postulate these and not other "capacities" for doing something--and not something else--in order to account for the observed behavior of physical things. In G. F. Stout's apposite statement: "As for our reason for classing dispositions as mental facts we may again refer to the analogous case of mass and energy. For the student of physics mass and energy are physical facts because for him their whole meaning and significance lies in their relation to material occurrences, the motions of bodies in space. Similarly, for the student of psychology dispositions are mental facts because for him their whole meaning and significance lies in their relation to consciousness and its various modifications."[19]

In short, we should not hesitate to attribute dispositions to ourselves provided that without such "structures" we cannot explain why it is that the "flow" of our consciousness takes one direction and not another. But neither can we postulate dispositions without ties to the conscious experience of persons. I have already urged that our conceptions of what takes place in our unconscious be guided by what we experience in consciousness (see chapter Two). It is important to warn ourselves constantly that there are no ideas or wishes being retained separately in the unconscious. For, as F. R. Tennant says, such status would have "all the attributes of their `conscious' equivalents, save that the subject is not only unaware of them, but also inactive in them." And this would be like saying that "there could be subconscious [unconscious] red, save that it was not a colour."[20]

4. In sum, I do not hesitate to postulate mental activities (dispositions) distinguished by their sensitivity to some and not other object-objectives. To be endowed with an unlearned disposition is to be "ready" to respond to a general "class" of objects in accordance with the objective or goal of that disposition. So, I suggest: if certain conditions are fulfilled, certain goal-seeking tendencies occur in my total experience that are definable by the kind

of objects that gratify them. Hence, the essence of a disposition or predisposition, consists in its selective pursuit of, in its differential focussing on, a similar object-objective in a variety of situations. (I shall usually use the word "predisposition" when I have unlearned, innate, disposition in mind. Most dispositions are learned. I am here trying to establish the case for primary, unlearned, telic dispositions.)

F.　In what sense are dispositions cognitive?

1. Assuming that this general account of disposition is on the right track, we must face the theoretical issue that lies beneath much of objection to instinct theory (and hence to primary motives and primary emotions). For the doctrine of innate tendency, and McDougall's view of instinct in particular, calls for an unlearned readiness to respond to an unlearned perceived situation. Clearly, an unlearned selective cognitive process is postulated (call it appraisal, or interpretation, or not) even though, in human beings especially, the "readiness" is subject to further learning and modification.

2. Before turning to a more specific defense of such predispositions, several remarks are in order. Those who talk "more objectively" about reflexes in which the response is geared to a given stimulus--the blinking of the eye when

an object approaches very closely and suddenly--somehow seem not to realize that they too are saying that, built into "the organism," are unlearned responses to certain stimuli which take priority over others.

Why is the question of prepotency for some stimuli any easier, theoretically, for the objective psychologist, who resists subjective words like "prepotent interpretation?" After all, on his view also the preparedness for some stimuli, and not others, is a given; that is, the preparedness is not in act but awaits a change in the total situation, before it is actualized. For the objectivist, also, learning presupposes some predispositions intrinsic to the agent, which allow for initial selective response. We may bury "prepotent perceptual interpretation" in the words "selective" and "capacity," but, theoretically, have we avoided the need for unlearned predispositions?

3. Moreover, is it theoretically more reasonable to place a predisposition in the organism than in the psyche? What is basically at stake, be it in the organic or in the psychic order, is the explanation of such continuities and changes that enable the agent to cope initially and successively with the ambient. Restricting ourselves to the personal level, we seem required to hypothesize dispositional "structures"--unpicturable, dynamic elaborations of the person's intrinsic nature. There seems no other unforced way of accounting for selective, meaningful experience at

the perceptual level, that is, for experience that sharply contrasts with what would have to be defined as unassimilated "pure" or "raw" data. As F. R. Tennant puts it: "The `meaning' evoked by a particular percept, is the expression in consciousness of the coming into activity of a system of dispositions."[21] Again, in Brand Blanshard's words: "...it is a striking fact about perception that our reading of what is given seems to be controlled not merely by what introspection can bring to light as present in consciousness, but also by the results of a great range of past experience, results which are not in consciousness at all."[22]

4. However, it is one thing to accept this general hypothetical conception of disposition to account for selective initial and continuous preparedness for response, and another to grant the use to which I shall put it to as I try to resolve the knotty issues surrounding unlearned or innate predisposition to perceive any object of a certain class (primary predisposition that I shall propose is in fact a primary emotion). Specifically, I am referring to essentially unlearned perceptual-conceptual responses in which both ability and urge (or "impulse") are so interconnected that the agent acts preferentially in certain situations--indeed the situation is as much defined by the urging as by the ambient.

I am aware that this shift from disposition to predisposition, within which unlearned cognition is one pole, arouses all the problems that psychologists in particular had hoped to leave behind as part of "speculative" philosophical baggage: innate ideas and a priori categories. But one dreadful ghost should no longer haunt us. Only a misguided zeal rejects innate motives (under whatever name) on the ground that they are necessarily tautologous--for example, that it is not explanation of war to say that there is an instinct of pugnacity.

There are tautologies and tautologies! All ultimates must be tautologous; that is, in serving as the basis for understanding other events, they themselves cannot be explained in terms of anything else. Thus, if it turned out on examination that there is an instinct to fight, expressed in a given, distinctive form of behavior, it would not succumb to the charge of vicious circularity if urge and behavior could not be explained as a form of some other unlearned urge. There may be no innate (unlearned) motives geared to definite behavioral patterns. But one is guilty of vicious tautology, or vicious circularity, only if he uses a general category to "explain" a specific form of action that in fact can be shown to be acquired.

For example, it is viciously tautologous for the physicist to rely on "electrical energy" to "explain" the burning of a particular electric light or the buzzing of a doorbell, but it is not vicious circularity to say that electricity _is_ what electricity does. For (presumably) it is this kind of energy, reducible no further, to which the physicist ultimately appeals as he explains all specific forms of physical change. Turning to psychology and the phenomena of learning, we see that G. F. Stout speaks to the point when he says: "If all intelligence is an after-effect due to prior learning by experience, we have no satisfactory account of the original processes in which the lesson is first learned."[23] And when he says: "The general capacity for being interested and attending is not an instinct,"[24] he is suggesting, if I may draw a parallel with electrical energy, that all instinctive responses instantiate this broader capacity that defines our purposive natures.

What, I take it, then, instinctivists have been proposing is that psychologists can reach psycho-physiological ultimates, that is, constitutive purposive orientations of the experient that ground his varied selective responses to the environment. Those who have rejected instincts and substituted non-purposive reflexes--do they not face the charge: tautology? For they are claiming: The physiological system is such that certain stimuli elicit certain responses; under normal conditions the knee jerks to certain stimuli. If we ask, why does it jerk? the answer is, because it jerks! If I am correct, the charge of tautology, is no more acceptable here then it is for ultimate psycho-physiological predispositions.

6. I have been arguing, generally, that the theory of innate motives in living beings is the attempt to define the nature of those purposive predispositions without which it is impossible to understand certain patterns of responding preferentially to some "classes of being" and not to others. But I would insist (following McDougall, in particular), that, as one moves up the evolutionary scale, the innate motives (including varying perceptual meanings) have also a greater degree of flexibility in the responses that can be made to the unlearned object(s). The lower the living beings are in the scale of evolution (and, among human beings, the less mature the person), the more rigid will the patterned mode of response be to the total situation that helps to define the predisposition. Thus, it cannot be emphasized strongly enough that whether a particular motivational disposition is innate or unlearned must always be left open to further debate. For evidence may always be found to show that a predisposition is actually derivative.

G.   Reflective overview

The further discussion of the relation of unlearned purposive predispositions in persons to emotions will take place as I elaborate, in the remainder of this book, the thesis that certain primary emotions _are_ primary predispositions--each to be differentiated as study reveals. A primary emotion _is_ the motivational predisposition inclusive of object-objective. Primary emotions are not epiphenomena of primary motives. We might call them emotive-conative predispositions. For as primary they are the unlearned, constitutive urges or tendencies in person-al existence.

I have given reasons for not appealing to physiological and behavioral "concomitants" as the necessary and sufficient clue to, let alone definition of, primary emotion. I shall emphasize the purposive thrust of "each" emotive tendency, _as_ consciously experienced, as the basis for hypothesized relation to the Body (that others can competently make). The person--whatever "correlates" are deemed reasonable in, say, the unconscious and Bodily realms--is such that certain situations are initially meaningful, as comprised in the primordial emotion, whatever modifications may be involved as he learns by interaction with his environments.

All this is intended to emphasize that factors in a person's regnant condition, in the Body and in the Environment, may in fact so change the situation as previously cognized that a different primary emotion occurs. For example, a situation that earlier elicited _primary sympathy_, may now, because the perceived-conceived meaning has changed, elicit _primary_ _anger_. But the primary emotion _is_ the predisposition; it _is_ the active tendency to realize certain object-ives intrinsic to the person's nature in relation to the Environment; seen from within, it _is_ a response to a context that allows the meaning expressed within the scope of its emotive activity-potential.

My central contention, then, is that an adequate theory of the person can no longer neglect primary emotions _as_ primary, predispositional, motives. This theory has many consequences, but basic among them is that no one, no society, can teach a human being to experience a primary emotion. Each person must himself undergo the original meaning-impetus to object-objective to begin with. If we do not begin with some emotive meanings, we are called upon to trace learned emotive complexes back to situations in which presumably there is zero-emotive meaning!

It is this skeletal contention that will take on flesh as I propose certain emotions as primary emotive dispositions, themselves unlearned, but subject to modification. My taking them up one by one does not mean that they exist in psychological, neatly labelled compartments. They are distinguishable foci of the unified being-becoming of the person.

Notes for Chapter Six

1. Harold B. Gerard, Contemporary Psychology, vol. 13 (12, 1968): 629.

2. Warren Shibles, Emotion (Whitewater, Wisconsin: Language Press, 1974). See the extensive bibliography and the critique of the reification of emotions--of which he would no doubt find an horrendous example in the view I am proposing.

3. Ibid., 21.

4. Ibid.

5. Peter A. Bertocci, "A Critique of G. W. Allport's Theory of Motivation," in Psychol. Rev., vol. 47 (1940): 501-532. See in the same issue (533-554) "Motivation in Personality: Reply to Mr. Bertocci," by G. W. Allport.

6. William James, The Principles of Psychology, vol. 2 (New York: Holt, 1896), 448.

7. Ibid., 442.

8. Alexander F. Shand, "The Source of Tender Emotion," chapter 16 of G. F. Stout's Groundwork of Psychology, 2d ed. revised by Robert H. Thouless, (London: University Tutorial Press, 1933), 176,177.

9. William McDougall, An Outline of Psychology (New York: Scribner's Sons, 1923), 110, italics added.

10. Ibid.

11. Ibid.

12. William McDougall, Organization of the Affective Life. A Critical Survey (Acta Psychologica), vol. 2 (1937): 320.

13. F. V. Smith, The Explanation of Human Behavior (London: Constable, 1951), 181.

14. William McDougall, ibid., 325.

15. Ibid., 326, italics added.

16. William McDougall, An Introduction to Social Psychology (Boston: Luce and Co., rev. ed., 1926), 51.

17. Ibid., 51, 52, italics added.

18. William McDougall, Outline of Psychology, 317. Space does not allow me to expand Drever's differences. See James Drever, The Instinct in Man (Cambridge University Press, 1917). especially 268; but the book as a whole, a constructive attempt to strengthen an essentially McDougallian conception, builds on this relative autonomy.

19. G. F. Stout, A Manual of Psychology, 3d ed, revised (London: University Tutorial Press, 1913), 25.

20. F. R. Tennant, Philosophical Theology, vol. 1 (Cambridge University Press, 1928), 114.

21. Ibid., vol. 1, 116.

22. Brand Blanshard, The Nature of Thought, vol. 1 (London: Allen and Unwin, 1939), 183.

23. G. F. Stout, <u>A</u> <u>Manual</u> <u>of</u> <u>Psychology</u>, 3d ed. revised (London: University Tutorial Press, 1913), 354.

24. Ibid., 357.

CHAPTER SEVEN

A Theory of Primary Emotions

In this chapter I deliberately argue the case for primary emotions by reference to the emotion <u>respect</u>. We shall thus be considering the kind of problem that faces this attempt to see in certain emotions the essence of human, unlearned, motivational predispositions.

A.   The primary emotion of respect as exemplar

1. Just as I cannot tell another person what the experience "yellow" is unless he experiences it, so I cannot tell him what "respect," as experienced, is. In both instances, what is learned is not the non-rational experience, but the name. In our sensory experiences we can usually point to something that "stays put," and thus facilitates agreement about the names we use. But when I use the word respect, though I myself have an experiential situation in mind which controls

the use of this word for me, I cannot be sure that a similar situation controls the use for another person.

Much hinges, in the view of primary emotion I am proposing, on the fact that the meaning intrinsic to the emotion experienced does not differ for "equally" sensitive experients. Thus, when I contend that respect is not to be conflated with fear, I may be confident that this distinction, that I express by "respect," is justified by the quality of my experience. Nevertheless, in a particular situation in which I experience respect, another may experience fear because the meaning of that situation is different for him.

Awareness of such difficulties should induce caution; but the difficulties should not be inflated into insuperable obstacles. Our concern, like that of Aristotle when he could not find a "good name" in current usage for a virtue, must be to indicate the situation for which we are using a word, preferably already in use, that seems a good fit.[1]

McDougall's description of a respect-situation illustrates the persistent difficulty I have in mind. For McDougall respect is not a primary emotion but an acquired sentiment, that is, a complex of emotions attached to a particular object. The opposite of respect is contempt. It will be clear from the following quotation that meaning is crucial as he distinguishes an emotive change in the shift from contempt to respect.

"Imagine a fellow-student toward whom you have been indifferent, or perhaps, inclined to be faintly contemptuous. He is ill-dressed, has few friends, and no outwardly sign of distinction. Then you discover that he is a student of unusual brilliance; that he has worked his way through college in face of great difficulties, perhaps is helping to support his mother at the same time, and that, before transferring to this college, he has run a mile in four minutes and thirty seconds. Your attitude becomes one of enduring respect, or even admiration. It is a sentiment of which the essential attitude is that of looking up to the object, the impulse is that of the submissive instinct; for he has shown, in certain regards, powers that are greater than your own. You have acquired an habitual deference or docility towards his opinion, admiration for his achievements, and respect for his personality as a whole."[2]

Our terminology is so loose that both the learned emotional complex--sentiment of respect--and the primary emotion, respect, can well afford the same name. But the controlling meaning that arouses respect is "powers interpreted as [more admirable] greater than your own." It is this meaning that accounts for the shift from contempt to respect. Obviously, this meaning can embrace many different actions and stances that are functionally equivalent for evoking respect. I am here expressing my difficulty --lurking in this description--in thinking of an emotion as an accompaniment of a tendency as opposed to itself being the tendency. The stress is on the fact that a certain meaning is the spearhead of the same emotive tendency that may actually be expressed in different conduct. It is that emotive tendency, that emotion, for which I would use the word respect even as I re-emphasize that this disposition is the same despite the differences in behavior. Accordingly, I would distinguish a kind of quality in submissive behavior (deference) born of respect, from submission born of another emotion, fear. I wish to capture that difference between emotive predispositions which, as I see it, forbids the emotion respect from being a derivative of fear, and forbids conflation of submissive behavior owing to fear with the deference arising from respect.

I am, in short, claiming the word respect for an emotion, not reducible to fear, and noting its inherent link with a certain meaning and kinds of response marked by deference "in thought and action" but not by submission of the sort associated with fear. Obviously, I wish to get beyond words to experiences and behavioral situations tied to different meanings; and I select the word respect as a better word than any other available to me. Elaboration for what may seem an arbitrary procedure is in order in this instance (that will be relevant to other primary emotions I shall propose).

2. I cannot capture the quality of the experienced emotion I am _naming_ respect. I am assuming that my readers and I mark significant differences between the emotion of respect and that of fear and of the meaning-situations that evoke each.

3. But why am I not content to identify respect with fear or a derivation from fear? As I have hinted, submissive _behavior_, broadly conceived, could as easily spring from fear as respect. An observer cannot be confident of the difference between "respectful deference" and "fearful submission," for much depends on the emotion dominating the experient in the situation. The situation involving _respect-deference_ as opposed to the situation involving fear-submission reflects _the_ _experient's_ _admiration_ for achievement, as judged by whatever standard _he_ uses. Another person, using a different standard, may experience fear-submission in the same circumstances. For example, what experienced teacher does not know the difference between students who "defer" (submit) from fear and those who defer from respect?

To summarize: it is the meaning evoked in a situation that determines the emotive predisposition that may or may not be carried out in behavior. Other things being equal, every time such a meaning is evoked, that particular emotion is experienced. And, be it carefully noted, the _meaning_ may be learned, _but the emotion that is geared to that meaning_ is not learned. For this reason the emotion is primary (unlearned, innate).

It is obvious that in support of this view I make my basic appeal to my reader's own inspection of what happens to him when, in certain situations, he experiences respect and when he fears. Does he roughly mark out, or distinguish, in his experience an emotive state that I am calling "respect?" If so, does he experience an impetus to defer to whatever, for him, means admirable? If he does, the word we decide to assign to it is an important but still quite secondary matter.

4. To continue, if I read my experience correctly, to feel respect is to experience the impetus to act out, to express the e-motion geared to its meaning-situation. Therefore, I do not assert, as McDougall does, that the emotion is the accompaniment of the underlying impetus. I do not experience this impetus except as this emotive impetus. When I am experiencing respect, I am experiencing the tendency to respond in a way that is deferential to some being I admire. I do not experience the tendency or impetus and the emotion; I experience the emotive-impetus that I call "respect."

5. In different terms, when I experience respect, I am in want: I desire to defer in some way that I consider appropriate at that time. Whether I actually express this desire, and how I do so, will depend on other factors in the

total situation as I perceive-conceive it (influenced by the forms of behavior for expressing respect already learned as acceptable in my social environment). But supposing that, owing to my ignorance of the "acceptable" deference, clumsy "misbehavior" results, <u>my inciting emotion remains respect -deference as long as I interpret the situation as admirable</u>. Hence, this emotion is an unlearned, telic predisposition dynamically riveted to meaning. This predisposition responds in characteristic, but not rigid, ways to certain "objects" deemed to be functionally equivalent in meaning as the person seeks gratification in his environments.

6. To expand on this "exemplar" emotive situation in more direct terms, the respect I experience is towards "an object"--an object admired for some reason as the meaning in that situation of "the object-ive" of the emotive tendency. That is, I cannot describe the emotion <u>respect</u> without confining myself to the object-objective that distinguishes it from other primary emotions. However, in undergoing respect for the pre-analytic object I may also reflectively "tease out" the way(s) in which object and objective are interrelated in this particular emotion. In sum, respect, as lived, endures as a telic tendency or predisposition intrinsically related to the object-meaning within the total situation I am undergoing. It is later articulation that distinguishes (not separates) the emotion, its objective,

and its object within the experience as a whole.

Again, in experiencing respect, I undergo the tendency, the incitement to actualize an objective as related to its object-meaning. As emotive tendency, it is a "becoming," in relation to the object-objective, that also seeks gratification usually but not necessarily in behavior. Moreover, my behavior may never express adequately the respect I experience. Hence, I must beware of identifying the emotive response with any specific behavioral pattern. For my behavior may be no more than a learned sign of, or a symbol of, the respect I experience towards the object -meaning.

Accordingly, each primary emotion needs to be inspected to bring to light its own "movement," or "crescendo," as it reaches the objective related to the object-meaning that may be said to "arouse" it in particular, and not another primary emotive tendency. It is only in an experienced context, in the drift of an emotion, that we tease out the meaning-pole, the objective without which we would not experience that emotion. Temporally we may experience a crescence that we call "the cause" of that emotional excitement. But post-mortem description must not tempt us to divide the emotive experience up into "three parts": emotion, its telic course, and its object-objective meaning. 7. I must now consider an objection of many respected contemporaries to any inner polar unity between object

-meaning and emotive-objective--that is, to the dynamic
unlearned tie between "cognitions" (meaning-poles) and
primary emotions. I would emphasize that what these
cognitions are in each primary emotion remains to be
determined in each instance.[3] I have been urging that
neither the cognitive pole nor the emotive pole is added to
the other, or fixed upon the other, through learning. Each
primary emotion requires as one pole the unlearned cognition
of meaning that distinguishes its object-objective as I move
to justify my selection of certain emotions as primary. The
warrant for this view will be more evident in each instance,
but perhaps I can allay some misunderstanding before going
further.

In order, at least, to clarify the cognitive
"preparedness" in telic predispositions that are governed by
meaning (and not reducible to, or identified with,
physiological and behavioral patterns), I suggest an analogy
with organic predispositions that must not be taken too
literally. In a biological context, we may think of the
body as an organic unity that is ready to act in certain
ways under certain conditions. Indeed, a given body can
hardly be defined apart from its own, unique, unlearned
preparations for some responses. Given this "prepared"
responsiveness, a body has a head-start in maintaining
itself as that body; in responding to the environment it
en-acts its predisposing, selective potential. Analogously,

in the psycho-physiological context of personal preparedness, I am proposing, for example, that the emotive predisposition of respect-deference is a selective activity -potential to respond in certain ways toward any existent deemed admirable by the person. I am opposing the setting aside of inspection and reasonable inferences favoring primary emotions--on the presupposition that only such unlearned preparedness (hence the only predisposition) is acceptable that is grounded in physiological and behavioral observation.

With respect-deference as our exemplar, I now advance general considerations that will act as guides in distinguishing an emotion as primary. I have purposely used respect-deference as an exemplar because it is not only difficult indeed to define it by behavior but also difficult to "locate" it physiologically. With this exemplar before us, I bring together the considerations central to this theory of primary emotions.

B.   The general nature of a primary emotion

1. A primary emotion is a telic predisposition aroused by a meaning that, unlearned, defines and guides the course of a person's seeking and response in his environmental situations. It is the total matrix, in which we distinguish

tendency to an object-meaning-objective, that comprises a primary emotion with its hedonic tone.

I share common ground with Arnold, Plutchik, and McDougall in holding that the responding agent is not simply triggered off by stimuli that are intrinsically meaningless to him as a living agent. Indeed, of the many factors in a total environment, those that become _psychic_ _stimuli_ to e-motive action have a distinguishable meaning for the pre -disposed agent. It is not enough to say that a person is so constructed that in the environmental press he finds himself never merely _for_ or _against_ certain stimuli. Actually, he responds to them as _differential_ _stimuli_ because _as_ _meanings_ they activate certain predispositions and not others. Thus, just as our stomachs digest certain things and not others, in accordance with their natures as stomachs, and whether or not we know the dynamics of digestion, so we as persons experience predispositional emotive responses in which we can, on reflection, discern a meaning-pole guiding the tendency as a whole.

2. The "empty mind" has no more to be said for it than the "empty" organism. And what I would stress now is that we should not await the discovery of some universal, organic locus for a primary emotion as the criterion for primacy --which is not to say that to know the locus is unimportant for full understanding of the way the emotion is related to, affects, and is affected by, organic states. We do

experience primary emotions--and respect-deference is a good example--that do predispose us to certain actions. Not to recognize their impact upon our experience, not to grant them a certain psychic autonomy, not to affirm that they are primary because we cannot point to physiological correlates, is to betray a bias about the relation of mind and body. Mental, psycho-physiological, and physiological predispositions cannot be denied because one holds some prior theory of mind and body. For our theory of mind-body should reflect our actual experience--in this case, our experience of emotions like respect-deference--rather than dictate even what should be regarded as evidence.

3. The search for primary emotions has been impeded by another contention, that one emotion may become another, or be brought into being by learning and environmental influence. The difficulties in distinguishing emotions, abetted by linguistic habits, encourage this bias. Thus we say: "My anger turned into fear," "Joy suddenly became sorrow or regret." But to talk thus, about one emotion becoming another, is to forget that in fact one primary emotion, far from becoming another, is only followed by another, because we have interpreted the situation differently. (Incidentally, who would not regard as preposterous the thesis that primary sensations, say blue and red, become such through learning?)

All the more, therefore, do we need to ask: What emotions, if any, are primary? And what conditions will predispose us toward certain emotive responses and not others? In pursuing a reasonable answer we do well to remind ourselves that we respond to ourselves in our environments by developing characteristics or patterns of behavior that are related to the meaning of the situation to us. For example, we do not respond with the emotion of gratefulness when we conceive a situation to be hurting a person, unless we think that situation will eventually produce worthwhile results. We do expect anger and not respect in certain meaning-contexts; sympathy and not fear in still others. In general, we are surprised when another person does not experience the emotion that we think a situation evokes. Yet, we may reflect: "If I were in his shoes and saw it as he does, I too would feel the same way (even if I would not allow myself to behave in that way!)."

Albeit, do we ever expect anger to be transformed into respect, sympathy to become fear? Hardly. Again, only as a situation takes on different meanings do we find one emotive complex "taking the place of" the other, along with relevant incipient or explicit behavior. In the last analysis, our emotions occur in contexts of meaning. And, I contend, it is important to know what meanings-within-emotive-predispositions we can expect of persons as a basis for teaching other orientations.

4. Not dependent on physiological changes or behavioral patterns alone, neither are emotions dependent on a prior appraisal of meaning as beneficial or harmful. (See the discussion of M. Arnold's view in chapter Five.) "Beneficial" and "harmful" do not help us to differentiate emotions from one another. And we are left with the problem: Why should the emotion be anger and not fear?

By contrast, my suggestion is that each primary emotion _is_ an emotive-meaning inherent in the sinew of a person's mental (or psycho-physiological) being. This emotive meaning and response form the intrinsic basis for the person's later evaluation of his situation in accordance with his controlling value-scheme. Insofar as any thinker defines a primary emotion, he will tell us what kind of behavior to expect, given the emotive-meaning. But the kind of linkage between experienced emotion, the specific behavior, and the particular physiological support is best left open for investigation. We cannot identify the emotion itself independently of the meaning-given-in-and-for-the -agent interacting with his ambient. If the meaning changes for the agent, the experienced emotion gives way to another for that very reason. The person may learn equivalents for the meaning-pole, and he may modify behavioral expression to suit the meaning, but the _tend_-ency of that emotion does not wax and wane in its telic thrust.

C.   The criterion for primary emotion

1. Implicit in what I have been saying about distinguishing
respect-deference as a primary emotion is the thorny
question: How shall we decide which emotions are primary (or
unlearned) if we yield the physiological foundation and
function as basic to the criterion of universality? Nothing
in what I have affirmed discourages or minimizes the
importance of searching for physiological, universal clues
to what persons experience. My protest is that the search
for such clues cannot be the sufficient criterion for
emotions as persons experience them--and no more so than can
particular behavior as such. As I select an emotion as
primary, I hope to show that the approach I am taking better
resolves certain issues that are otherwise, as I have
already partly suggested, left in the air. To that end I
continue to use respect-deference as my exemplar.

2. I can refer to nothing beyond my emotions as experienced
for the qualitative differentia of one emotion from that of
any other. The quality of an emotion is as hard to
"isolate" as is the quality of a sensory datum; but we can
only know this by trying to inspect what is present in
consciousness as carefully as possible. As I have already
granted, I can no more tell another what the experienced
quality of respect is than I can tell him what the quality
of yellow is. But I can "point to," intimate, the kind of

experience I have in mind by referring to contrasts-in
-situation. I can say: "When you experience respect, you
experience the impulse to submit, to defer, to the "object"
you admire--but not as you defer or submit when you
experience fear." We do indeed often disagree about the
meaning of the object, but once we do agree we experience
the impetus of respect-deference, although we may express it
differently.

Still, in the last analysis, I must revert to my basic
claim: I can discover in the emotion, respect, no hint of
fear; and elation or gratitude may flicker in and out of the
emotional field as the meaning-focus changes. To be sure, I
cannot be too confident about my introspection. And I can
understand how one, gazing at submissive behavior, might see
similarities between fearful and deferential behavior. But
when someone tells me that respect, as lived, is "really"
fear--or any other emotional quality--I can only say no,
invite him to look again, and look again myself.

3. Sticking by the experience I have pointed to, I go on to
ask: If respect-deference is not primary, from what other
emotion or emotional compex could it arise? I have already
objected to a psychological alchemy that would allow
respect, for example, to arise from fear. But another
watershed confronts us.

It is often contended that, given certain universal
organic needs, secondary "needs" can be developed owing to

environmental influences and learning. Analogously, it is suggested that from certain presumably primary emotions others can be derived through a learning process. We are now to envision a psycho-physiological being who, say, has no pre-disposition to respect, but who, given primary fear, can be taught to develop respect by redirecting, or modifying, the expression of fear. Once this alternative is carefully stated, we can see that much is being demanded from the process of "developing, "modifying," and "deriving" one kind of experience from another. I suggest that the answer is not as obvious as seems to be assumed; that, in this instance, my counter-claim that respect cannot develop from fear, or be derived from it, be a serious option.

I am aware that important theoretical and practical motives sway, and should sway, decisions in favor of derivation owing to learning. A particularly strong motive favoring derivation (and thereby restricting lists of innate tendencies), is the conviction that, by changing environmental influences and directing learning, we can free ourselves from the established behavior originating from our supposedly consitutive predispositions.

It will be recalled that I have emphasized the person's plasticity in his modes of expressing primary emotions. Indeed, I should argue that, as the person acquires habits, attitudes, sentiments, traits and self-concept, he himself influences the course of his primary emotives as he interacts with his ambience. However, granted such learning as critical to the individual and social expression of primary motives, I suggest that we still must ask, for example: Can a parent _teach_ a child respect, if, by definition, the child can experience only fear, anger, and bodily needs? My answer must remain no. Any other answer, I suggest, may well be confusing the behavioral response with the emotive-meaning actually inspiring it.

4. I can understand that a parent in a certain culture can teach a child to _behave_ in a certain way: "Say `Sir' and `Ma'am' to your elders!" Such behavior can be taken either as submission born of fear or deference born of respect. But if we, arguing from derivation, say that respect is a form of fear, are we even close to correct in supposing that deferential behavior is really fear in modified expression?

But suppose the motive-emotion is respect. The resulting behavior might be the same. Is it submission or deference? Before we answer, we do well to ask whether the relation of father to son is the same if the deferential behavior involved is grounded in respect rather than fear? On this view I suggest, the father may arouse both; the child can submit or defer as he interprets his meaning-relation to his father as calling for fear or for respect. The fear may be modified, the respect may be modified, but does fear ever become respect?

The upshot of what I am suggesting is that a parent, a society, cannot teach a child to respect, to experience a primary emotional concrescence, if it cannot teach him those meanings that will call forth respect rather than fear in him. The child may, to be sure, submit to another out of fear; still, the "same" behavior can express more than one emotive-meaning. It is very important to know which emotion is being expressed, for the child who behaves respect-fully toward his parent has a different total response from that of the child who feels fear and behaves "with deference."

In sum, I am suggesting that too often, in the name of "environmental influence," or "learning," we are told that emotions can be changed or transformed without the realization that such statements rest not on experience but on an appeal to emotional alchemy. It is one thing to say that the emotion that is related to one object can be extended to other objects that have acquired a similar meaning by learning (that my fear of rats may be extended to squirrels and chipmunks); it is another to say that the emotive response itself can be transformed into any other, or derived "by learning" from it.

4. If these considerations carry any weight at all, we do well to re-open the case for enlarging the list of primary emotions in the interests of adequate education. For in educational practice it makes all the difference in the world whether we are dealing with persons who have three or

four primary e-motives, or a larger number, upon whose dynamics we can proceed to develop our ends and means of education. To restrict ourselves again to our exemplar, if we assume that "respectful" behavior is always a form of fear, then our problem is to "make a child respectful" by appealing, however subtly, to his fears. The child who says: "Sir" (as one possible sign of respect), because his response is linked with fear of punishment, may indeed come to make a dependable, "polite" response in specific situations. But such behavior, even should it become so deeply ingrained as to be "second nature," is still a form of fear-response. But should it be the case that respect is another primary root of "deferential" behavior, before us open alternative ways of teaching foundations of social behavior. For example, the kind of responses that many people, young and old, make to customs and institutions differs accordingly as they experience fear for what is imposed by sheer might upon their weakness, or by respect for the institutions whose purposes they appreciate. A family ruled by fear is not a family based on respect, or even on a reasonable "mix" of both.

5. Much is said about "education for emotional development." But the very belief that in order to "produce" respect--or any emotion whatsoever--all we need is appropriate environmental pressure, tends to devalue the product as something purely contingent and "man-made." It makes a

difference whether we think that an emotion like sympathy, or tenderness, or wonder, is primary, instead of derived by nurture from "more fundamental emotions." Moreover, in "educating emotions" we shall concentrate not only on expression or behavior but on meaning also. Adequate learning will call for appropriate accommodation of an emotion to the situation in which it may be expected to arise, and it will take into account the effects that such accommodation will have on others within a society and culture. Thus, the individual experiencing respect may well need to learn what is allowable in his total interaction with others. But the training of this and other emotions will now involve sensitive response to a larger horizon of meanings; it will not suffice to appeal to "survival value" interpreted in biological terms alone.

It remains to stress that, as this discussion of respect indicates, in persons the expression of a primary emotion will vary as the individual's capacity to see the intent and consequences of those expressions of respect and deference in the context of his relation to his family and relevant social institutions. It would be unusual for a person, as his status changes, not to move from "accepted" patterns of "showing respect" to patterns that express his own more individualized appreciations of the kind of behavior that respect for those he admires involves.

D.   Reflective overview

Our discussion of primary emotive predispositions, as we shall continue to see, reveals not only intrinsically thorny problems but also presuppositions that obstruct our vision of emotion in the experience of persons. In particular, apart from preconceived views of the mind-body problem, and of the methodological dogmatism of scientism, nothing, I suspect, has prejudiced the interpretation of emotions in persons more than the hasty conclusions drawn from the evolutionary resemblances observed by some paleontologists, embryologists, and by some students of comparative anatomy.

Thus Tinbergen in The Study of Instincts, says: "Man is an animal. He is a remarkable and in many respects a unique species, but he is an animal nevertheless. In structure and functions of the heart, blood, intestine, kidneys and so on, man closely resembles other animals, especially other vertebrates....Man and the primates have only recently diverged from a common primary stock."[4] By themselves such statements are harmless, although they are made with an air, frequently, of having at last put man where he belongs. The assumption is made that because physiological structures are alike, conscious experiences, including emotions, may also be expected to be alike.

My basic contention all along has been that, however necessary psycho-bio-chemical and behavioral observations

are to an adequate understanding of personal agency, we
cannot deny ourselves the data available to us only in the
experience of self-conscious persons. We have allowed
ourselves to be so intimidated by the supposed inaccuracies
of introspection that we have trusted our inspection of
conscious experience only to the extent to which it was
bolstered up by physiological and behavioral accounts--as if
these did carry labels to be translated (almost without
interpretation) by the informed observer. Could the rat,
the cat, the seal, and the chimpanzee tell us what they
experienced as they coped with problems, would we disregard
their report? Would we have gained nothing by noting what
they reported as consciously experienced, granted the
different degrees or levels of cognitive appreciation of
themselves and their world?

In any case, as I proceed to propose certain emotions as
primary predispositions I shall examine each as it is
consciously experienced as the basis for understanding the
kind of difference it makes to our view of the dynamics of
unlearned motivation in persons.

Notes for Chapter Seven

1. Aristotle, _Nicomachean_ _Ethics_, Book IV, for example, 1220a.

2. William McDougall, _Outline_ _of_ _Psychology_ (New York: Scribner's Sons, 1923), 424.

3. John T. MacCurdy remarks: "Turn to almost any textbook of psychology and you will see a problem stated in terms of many different emotions, but the answer given in terms of one." _Psychology_ _of_ _Emotion:_ _Morbid_ _and_ _Normal_ (New York: Harcourt Brace, 1925), 41.

4. From Nikolaas Tinbergen, _The_ _Study_ _of_ _Instinct_ (Oxford: Clarendon Press, 1950), 205, as quoted in Ronald Fletcher: _Instinct_ _in_ _Man:_ _In_ _the_ _Light_ _of_ _Recent_ _Work_ _in_ _Comparative_ _Psychology_ (London: Allen and Unwin, 1957).

CHAPTER EIGHT

Primary Emotions: Sex and Organic Needs

Any primary emotion, I am proposing, is a distinguishable, emotive predisposition defined by the meaning-object discernible in its personal matrix. In this chapter, I turn to primary emotions that can be localized more definitely in particular organic processes. However, I shall contend that they cannot be understood in human experience in terms of organic activities alone. I refer to sex, hunger, thirst, and "organic needs" like sleep and exercise.

A.   Lust-sex

1. The primary emotion, lust-sex, provides illuminating contrast to respect-deference. There is universal agreement as to its innateness, and it can be "located" physiologically. Lust-sex involves unlearned sensory-perceptual meaning, and by learning it can be attached to

many objects that become sexual equivalents to the primary object-objective. I am aware of the derogatory connotations the word lust has for many persons, but I purposely would free it from negative connotations in favor of the more inclusive meaning, as in "lust for life." As with the respect-deference, so here, and with other primary emotions, by placing the emotion-word first, I am emphasizing my thesis that it is the inner emotive thrust that is "directive" of the action and behavioral aspects of the particular emotion; the hyphen suggests the objective pole, needing more specification in each instance.[1]

Lust-sex is the emotion experienced by a person as a qualitative impetus whose meaning-objective is usually a member of the opposite sex deemed attractive in ways that facilitate sexual advances and intercourse. That this definition must be broad in terms of the object-objective of lust will become evident. Many writers assume that the reader will readily know what is involved in lust-sex, but it is no easy matter to stipulate what its meaning is in human experience. For here in fact is an emotion whose meaning-pole is not necessarily restricted by reference to the opposite sex and whose gratifying action, or means of expression, is quite variable.

2. Were we to speak only biologically, the physiological nucleus could be defined with relative ease, and the goal "procreation" be acceptable. But lust in persons is an

emotion that can be directed toward persons of the same sex, the opposite sex, "surrogates" like animals and other "objects." The restriction of the goal to procreation is probably the result of thinking of sex in persons largely as the extension of biological conceptions about instinct in animals. However, the sexual behavior of animals, in contrast to that of persons, shows little flexibility in the mode of behavioral expression. In persons, once we focus on lust-sex as experienced, once we note that the initiation, crescence, and fulfillment of the emotion can take so may behavioral, imaginary, and symbolic forms, we realize that the problem of definition is much more complex. Certainly, the goal of lust-sex as experienced cannot be restricted to procreation. The above definition is intended to focus on the emotion experienced by a person in his varied and variable behavioral and mental responses to the object that has lustful meaning to him.

This focus is consonant with the comment made by Ruth and Edward Brecher as they introduce the influential study by W. H. Masters and V. E. Johnson, The Human Sexual Response (1966). In their words: "A sexual relationship between a man and a woman can have deep psychological overtones. Poets and novelists have portrayed these emotional factors in all their richness, so that almost all of us are aware of the psychological interplay of love and affection, ego satisfaction, the need for security and the fascination of novelty, the pleasures of mutual play, the joy of giving and receiving."[2]

3. Whatever our difficulties with Sigmund Freud's epochal work, we are indebted to Freud for trying to express the nuclear intent of sex in his theorizing about the dynamics of _libido_ and _id_. No "simple" drive this toward some clearcut pre-ordained unravelling of an emotive process! Indeed, for Freud the libido (id) seemed often to become identical with the desire to live and to live as pleasurably as possible.[3]

Once sex is seen as the demand for pleasurable expression of functions related to inlets and outlets of the body, and to mother and father as means for assuring pleasurable gratification, it is not difficult to extend the scope of sex to infantile and pre-pubescent sexuality and to include in its goal mother and father (or surrogates). Yet from Freud's work and from the history of the interpretation of the very broad meaning of this urge, we should learn to avoid a conception of innate tendency that is so broad that other different drives or motives become derivations of it.

In short, once we ask what the primary emotion, lust-sex, involves, we must be more restrictive without losing variability in expression. Perhaps I can "fence in" the experienced character of lust-sex with adequate cognizance of its flexibility in expression.

4. I have already suggested that lust-sex is a psycho
-physiological predisposition related to an objective,
usually involving a member of the opposite sex, who is
perceived (at least) as a "partner" in releasing and
gratifying the tension experienced. I shall here not enter
into the question of the nature and importance of mutual and
harmonious sexual expression at climax--the whole
controversy at this point testifying to the difficulty of
defining sex in biological terms alone. Suffice it to note
that, commenting on the investigations of Masters and
Johnson, the Brechers write: "Rather, we see orgasms for
women as well as men, as an essentially physiological phase
of human response to sexual stimulation. Without it, the
experience is impoverished. With it, the entire experience
from first stirrings of desire to ultimate satisfaction and
resolution can be enjoyed in all its richness....we are
aware of no accounts of women who, once they have learned to
experience it, prefer the sexual experience without its
physiological climax."[4] Obviously, such comments are hardly
intended to end all controversy.

In the midst of current controversy, I would suggest that
so much recent literature--some of it in the name of
scientific sexology--has prescribed certain patterns of
physiological response as the proper way to achieve
satisfying sexual experience. Many readers have been led to
believe that sexual "technique" is the highway to sexual

satisfaction. What might be called the "athletics of sex" expresses ludicrous extremism. Thus, some of the very attempts that were to liberate us from the anxieties of a supposedly rigid, Puritan ethic have created new anxieties related to sexual performance. For the uncompromising "will of God" we have substituted a pattern of the sexual response in our loins.

5. Irving Singer,[5] with such works as Masters' and Johnson's in mind, has reviewed methods of acquiring data, and concluded that there is no neat or fixed correlation between any one pattern of physiological response and sexual satisfaction--either between partners, or within the life of any male or female. Singer, accordingly, overthrows the tyranny of fixed physiological frameworks for sexual satisfaction. He is not even willing to prescribe what he, on the whole, seems to favor: a harmonizing of the clitoral -vulval and of the uterine orgasm.

Singer's own analysis, as I see it, suggests a conclusion that he does not draw, probably because his concern is to stay close to what can be confirmed by physiological observation. The fact is, as he knows, that a rich tradition insists that human beings find enduring and meaningful quality in sexual experience only as their sexual experience becomes also a way of symbolizing and celebrating the other meanings and values they seek. Thus, persons who caringly love each other do not minimize the sensuous and passionate gratifications in their responses to each other. But such persons, finding much of the meaning of their lives through each other, develop their own physiological patterns of mutual response in a way that expresses and symbolizes the quality of their commitment to each other.

I would conclude: without for a moment minimizing the sensuous and passionate gratifications of physiological sexual episodes, we need to center on the fact that the experience of lust-sex takes place in persons as part of their search for meaning and value. The "secret" to human sexuality may begin in, but never ends with, patterns of sexual response.[6] I would stress that the quality of what may be referred to as a psychic climax, with or without organic features, depends upon the interpretation given by the experient to the gratifying situation. Such quality may range from the quality of pleasure experienced when lust is gratified largely as an end in itself to the quality experienced when different meanings are expressed in the behavior that brings gratification. In any case, lust-sex is not love; when love is involved, sexual quality in the experience of persons is influenced by the quality of the love that the expression of lust-sex symbolizes.

Accordingly, there is scope for lust-ful gratification at different levels and in different ways, including masturbation and other means of self-stimulation. I should want to apply the same considerations to homosexuality--

without entering into the question of its innateness. (I
bear in mind that sexual behavior, homosexual or
heterosexual, may not spring from the demand for sex-
expression.) My main concern here is to emphasize that
whatever the physiological bases of sex, whatever the
behavior, the "sexual" factors involved reflect meaning as
perceived by the individual at a given stage in the
development of his personality.

6. No one can define lust in a way that conveys meaning to a
person who has not experienced it. Here, again, we assume
potentiality and predisposition for the experience with its
crescendo and diminuendo. What person can confidently tell
another, or even himself, apart from the actual experience,
the qualities he perceives as attractive in the object
-objective of his emotive impetus? For, once more, there is
not first a stimulus and then an emotive response; the
object is definable only in the context of the polar,
emotive thrust. De gustibus non disputandum means in this
connection that the "objective" situation, as a lust
-potential one, need not be interpreted by two persons in
the same way. (Indeed, if psychologists and sociologists
are to make a case against other primary emotions because of
difficulty in finding a necessary and universal pattern of
behavior, then they should, in view of observable
variability of behavioral sexual response, drop sex from
their list of unlearned motives.)

7. The complexity and variability of lust-sex-expressions in

persons provide the occasion for emphasizing the flexibility in the means for expressing the same end in the life of any "instinct" (primary emotion) in persons. Indeed, this flexibility in any instinctive expression in persons was so completely overlooked by many of McDougall's critics that he was led in Energies of Men to change his terminology from instinct to propensity. As he said, "while in the animals (especially the lower animals, as we have seen) certain abilities function in close connection with certain propensities, such connections in man are loose and variable, one aspect and condition of his great general plasticity.[7] It is still the case, to be sure, that in the sexual propensity there is a closer gearing of a more specialized group of native abilities than there is, for example, in respect-deference. But, generalizing from its first appearance until late in life, there is flexibility in the means of expressing the emotive impetus; and much always depends on the interpretation of situations in which it appears.

8. Thus, lust-sex helps us to see again that persons, in their complex unity, are gripped by a total internal -external meaning-situation in which they discover dimensions of their own natures, actual and potential--and always within an environmental context to which their emotive predispositions make their own selective contribution. Hence, we do not properly speak of the

person's environment <u>and</u> his emotion: it is <u>his</u> environment as involving that emotive selectivity.

At the same time, since the experience and expression of lust-sex takes place in a unitary person who can experience other primary emotions, as well as derivative "fusions," there is in him a ferment that "contributes" to, "challenges," "threatens," a chosen direction he has given his life. No more than any other emotion can lust-sex live a life of its own. Its total meaning and value will depend on its interrelation with other factors and emotions operative in his personal development. Nevertheless, we must avoid speaking as if lust-sex could be given outright value in a life only because of its connection with other emotions and needs. Lust-sex has its physiological correlations and its relatively autonomous rhythm, hedonic tone, and unique quality, to contribute to the matrix of personal being-becoming. At the same time, difficult as suppression (and unfortunate as repression) may be, it is simply contrary to fact to attribute to lust-sex a <u>necessarily</u> important, let alone dominant, place in any person's life.[8]

9. The inherent plasticity of lust-sex has consequences for sex education that demand at least passing emphasis here. The child, adolescent, and adult needs to discover what is involved in experiencing and expressing his psycho-physiological tension in relation to arousing situations.

For example, an adolescent may not know that caressing of the other person will lead to heightening of sexual tension. He needs to learn about his own psycho-physiological rhythms, about the conditions that incite his own lustful responses and about the many permutations and sequences he may expect, including those rooted in his past experiences. The inciting "object" is so often both the imagined and the ongoing behavior. In sum, a person is a learner about the power and the meaning of lust-sex in his own total development. Sex information, let alone sex education, is hardly a luxury for persons.

B.   Hunger and other organic needs.

1. I have been proposing that unlearned, emotive tendencies toward ends can be distinguished within the complex context of the person's activity-potentials. The presentation of respect-deference and lust-sex, certainly offering a contrast in physiological dependence on localization, supports my thesis that the clue to each primary emotion is in conscious human experience, whatever its correlations add to our fuller knowledge of its dynamics. Can this thesis about primary emotions be extended to a number of predispositions that might be called bodily or "organic needs," namely, hunger, thirst, and the need for rest,

sleep, and for exercise? These organic needs are commonly regarded as universal.

2. The needs just mentioned do fall under McDougall's description of an unlearned propensity as generating "when it is stirred, stimulated, or excited, an active tendency which may operate at any level in the scale of consciousness or awareness, from the most self-conscious level to one of which the most skilled and the most willing efforts of introspection, or of retrospection, fail to render any account."[9]

Interestingly enough, McDougall classifies coughing, sneezing, breathing, evacuation, under "very simple propensities subserving bodily needs."[10] But he names no emotion accompanying either these or the "bodily needs" they serve. At one time he suggested *gusto* as the emotion attending food-seeking; but, in the end, he stated no emotions as accompanying either the main bodily needs or the "very simple propensities."

I find myself not firmly committed to considering these unlearned, "bodily" needs--hunger, thirst, rest, sleep, exercise--to be emotions, but neither am I convinced that we cannot distinguish an emotive tendency that constitutes the thrust of each. For a while I was tempted to follow McDougall's constructive disciple, James Drever, and set, alongside of full-fledged propensities, "specific `appetite' tendencies" which have tension such as might be expected in the rudimentary states of more primitive conscious beings. Hunger, thirst, nausea, the need for exercise, rest, and sleep do not wait upon an external stimulus (as instincts presumably do in his view), and they do involve an uneasiness and tension.[11] Drever does hint that a primitve level of emotion might also be present. But for him, as for McDougall, emotion is not the conative or appetitive tendency itself.

3. I have already argued, however, that the contention that an emotion accompanies a presumably non-emotive tendency still leaves us with the problem of explaining the telic quality of that specific emotion as well as the (relative) autonomy of that emotive tendency. Emotions involve responses to meaning as nuclear to their own being. Each primary emotion is the persisting process, qualified by some hedonic or unhedonic tone. However, if, like McDougall, I cannot name a unique emotion for each of these "organic" predispositions, why, indeed, not settle for Drever's "appetite tendencies," with uneasiness and tension as well as hedonic tone and "primitive emotion" as a possible accompaniment?

If I did so settle I could avoid what must seem, in my list of primary emotions, tour de force. But, admitting more than a little uncertainty, I persist in rejecting the view that these organic tendencies are in essence devoid of emotive quality. In persons are these physiological predispositions simply overlaid with cognitive, hedonic, and emotive accompaniments? Or are they integral to persons who, from infancy onward, learn to adjust them in the process of coping with their environmental situations?

4. I am not competent to deal with genetic and comparative aspects in the development of cognitive and emotional life. My concern, nevertheless, is that our model for interpreting "stages" of human experience should allow us to find our way, without miracle, from the infantile to adolescent and adult forms of cognition and emotion.

What so often happens, on the purely physiological view of bodily needs such as those referred to above, is that words like "tension" and "uneasiness" are used to suggest emotion when there is no human experiential analogue to what is actually intended. Words like "tension" and "uneasiness" convey meaning only by borrowing from emotive quality and hedonic tone as persons experience these. I ask myself: To what do these very words refer in terms of purely bio -chemical or physiological processes?

I opt therefore for the following alternative: "organic tensions" _are_ emotive hedonic tendencies; each has its own object-objective emotion distinguishable at a different level of experience. I must immediately grant that I do not have an emotion-_word_ for what we experience when we hunger, or thirst or experience the want for sleep and exercise (to limit myself to these). But I ask: Would careful inspection of these tendencies, as lived, leave us unable to report that each _is_ distinguishable by its own distinctive emotive -hedonic qualities? I, for one, have no difficulty distinguishing the emotive-hedonic states involved when I want food and drink (at the level of hunger and thirst), and when I am "in want of" exercise or sleep. After all, a person who knows nothing about the physiology of these urges does not readily confuse what he wants. His "uneasiness," "excitement," or "disturbance," _is_ hunger-uneasiness, thirst -uneasiness, discriminable as emotive-hedonic tendencies whose physiological correlates are more readily inferred. In each instance he is experiencing a qualitative regnancy in his psycho-physiological being (included his lived-body).

5. My thesis here brings us back almost with a vengeance to the relation of the mental to the bodily dimensions in human experience. For example, when I say "I need sleep," my organic situation, as viewed by a physiologist, may not conform to the physiologist's criterion of conditions for Physiological Sleep (and Rest). At the same time, physiologists can provide drugs that put me to sleep or "sedate" me and induce Rest (even if I, on regaining consciousness, do not feel what _I_ _mean_ by "rested"). Again, a doctor tells a person that he must eat. But the person experiences no "want to eat." We cannot somewhat hastily paper over, by referring to "psycho-somatics," the relations and interrelations involved at the personal level. But if

we focus on meaning, we are more likely to keep before us both the situation as experienced and also as observed in Electrical, Chemical, and Physiological terms. In any case, there is nothing to be gained by treating these emotions (in which sensori-motor factors clearly play an important part in the lived-experience and lived-body) solely as accompaniments of disturbances that take place completely outside of the lived-experience and lived-body. For the fact is that the person who reports, on the basis of his lived-state: "I'm hungry," "I need sleep," does experience a distinguishable differential, an emotive-hedonic state that may or may not have roots in the Body.

I am not claiming that these "organic" emotive-hedonic states are not usually instigated by conditions in the Body. But intent as I am on "saving the appearances," I claim that these emotive-hedonic tendencies, nameable or not, are experienced not as adjuncts; they have, as it were, a psychic power of their own; a power, indeed, that expresses the total personal being at that time in that situation.

This view is consistent with Magda Arnold's comment: "While the impulse to find food is originally mediated by relays from the lateral hypothalamus, it is intensified by the sensation of hunger, which is aroused by hunger pangs."[12] Hunger as experienced is not identical with the thalamic state; and, as defined in persons particularly, this fact should be noted. Nor would I deny "that hunger is aroused by receptors in the hypothalamus that detect the lack of various substances in the blood,"[13] for this is one important level of description that traces the awareness of hunger-emotion to physiological changes. But I must mildly protest the reference to receptors in the hypothalamus that "detect" the lack of various substances in the blood. It is unwitting reliance on such questionable analogies that leads to identifying hunger with physiological changes, rather than with a hunger-emotion that may or may not include those changes. Arnold comes close to this view when she says: "Hunger, like emotion, seems to be a tendency to action based on the appraisal of something as unpleasant....Hunger seems to urge us toward food."[14]

6. A similar notation by Arnold suggests a further comment. She writes: "After the first hunger is stilled, the thought may occur to a man to stop eating; but if the meal is appetizing _or if he is too intent on the pleasure of taste_, he may go on eating until the increasing distension of the stomach is felt as unpleasant."[15] The italicized portion should serve to remind us that the emotive-hedonic complex, initiated by one meaning within a given context, may take on a new meaning without a change in the organic-behavioral context. This "switch" from "first hunger" to "taste-appetizing" should serve to warn us again that _it is important to know the meaning-context within which any emotion is experienced_. Otherwise we may assume that the

same emotion is being "channelized," "redirected," or "sublimated," when in fact that emotion has been supplanted by another because the meaning has changed.

This point is worth further emphasis. For it is not unusual to read that hunger, thirst, or sex, is being redirected, or "sublimated," into aesthetic and religious dimensions when indeed the initial emotion has vanished. The fact in personal experience is that supposed purely "organic needs"--"hunger," "thirst," "sleep," "rest," and "sex," for example--continue to be used in contexts in which there is little or no resemblance to the originative appetitive emotions. It would probably be truer to say that eating, drinking, being at rest, sexual experiencing continue symbolically into streams of aesthetic and religious experience that are distantly related, if at all, to the initiating meaning.

In sum, it is all too easy to assume that once we have provided the physiological description, or indicated the sheer survival value of "basic needs," we have told the "fundamental" story. Hence, hunger and thirst, and "demands for survival and self-maintenance," instead of being important phases of the meaning of personal survival, become the ruling (organic) paradigm. Too frequently scholars interpret the dynamics of "biological" evolution by leaving the personal out to begin with, and then explaining the personal as extensions of the organic!

C.   Reflective overview

1. My underlying thesis is that the dimensions of personal experiencing can either be actually distinguished in consciousness or inferred as related to them. We cannot close the question about needs that may not be emotive-hedonic even though they are constitutive phases of the personal whole. The person, in the model I suggest, _is_ all of _his_ dimensions, and even at "the survival level" he has all the potential assets and liabilities of personal being, however rudimentary and episodic they are _as_ _personal_. To speak of a person living "like an animal" can be more mischievous than we realize. When a person tries to be an animal he is likely to be "worse" than any animal we know.

2. This whole matter raises many questions, not the least those concerning the nature of "personal being" in what we consider extremes, be it in embryo, in infancy, or in senility. We find ourselves thinking of a person in the last stages of a withering illness--sedated, intravenously fed, oxygenated--as a "mere vegetable." There is little doubt that telic processes still go on, even though nothing of "the person and personality we know" is still there, any more than it was there at conception or in infancy. But such poles and deviations, I suggest, are still to be examined in relation to the personal and not as a "return"

to the "animal." Again, if we are to use the conception of
evolutionary continuity either as a movement from animal to
human, or from infant to adult, then we must do so in such a
way that the human and adult remains understandable without
appeal to undefined factors in an assumed process of
evolutionary change.

I have chosen, therefore, to regard "organic" needs or
appetitive tendencies (that are essentially preservative of
personal being specifically in bodily-Bodily dimensions) as
distinguishable primary emotions that move to fulfillment,
each as a particular complex in the development of a person.
If I am told that I am stretching the word "emotion," I can
only suggest that phrases like "hardly or barely alive," or
"low level of energy," are even less helpful, for they tend
to encourage us to forget that we are dealing with forms of
the personal rather than of the biological as such.

3. These reflections are not inconsistent with the
metaphysical view that a person is ultimately a hierarchical
system of psychic cells or monads. On this account, the
telic work of the "organism" could be understood as the
interacting of a society of psychic cells, each with its own
unique aim. The Physiological description of their
activities would be an abstractive description serving the
goals of biological science. The view of primary emotions I
am proposing here does not depend, however, on whether the
ultimate entities of the body are Leibnizian monads,

Whiteheadian actual occasions, Democritean atoms, chemico
-physical fields of force, or bio-chemical cells. The
personal experience of emotion, be it hunger, sex, respect,
or sympathy, must not be seen simply as a derivative from
any "forces" defined without reference to emotion as
experienced. All the more, however, must primary emotions
be constantly subjected to more sensitive inspection. For
emotions, as predispositions activated by meaning-objects
that "pull" the person toward their objectives, are
"initiated" in situations whose full meaning in the life of
a person is not immediately clear.

Never were the words of James Ward more fitting: "we
cannot imagine the beginning of life but only life begun."[16]
What we begin with is a person already living, on the go,
becoming experienced by working out whatever cognitive
hedonic-emotive thrusts he is undergoing at different stages
of maturity, in an environment of persons and their
institutions, among the ways of nature.

4. Finally, once we recognize adequately the centrality of
meaning to the very existence and quality of an emotion, and
once we realize that a psychological alchemy underlies the
notion of transforming one emotion into others, we face the
task of defining at least those emotions that prima facie
seem irreducible and universal. In the last chapter, I
purposely used respect-deference as the exemplar of a theory
of primary emotions that resists reduction of any primary

emotion to any other emotion, because it is difficult or impossible to point to physiological correlates.

In this chapter, the focus has been on motives that are more localizable physiologically and that nobody denies to be universal. The sexual urge lends itself more readily to the view that its essential nature is emotive. The plasticity of modes of expression within the basic objective of lust-sex shows that neither some specific behavioral pattern nor the Physiological correlate can account for the variety of human sexual response. We also noted that in human experience the quality of lust-sex, as of other primary emotions, will be influenced by the other meanings and values that are sought by the person engaged in defining the "meaning of life" for himself.

When I suggest that unlearned motives like hunger and thirst--again localizable physiologically--are in essence primary emotions, I seem to be definitely in trouble. For much of what occurs in these predispositions seems to go on without reference to the personal meaning, and their patterns of response are so much more definitely linked to inner and outer behavioral factors. Nevertheless, if meaning is as significant as it so often seems to be in initiating and guiding these "organic" motives, may we not reasonably include them among our primary emotions? For, granted the importance of physiological processes open to our gaze, these processes remain phases of the total, emotive wholes of meaning experienced as hunger-emotion and thirst-emotion.

Moreover, I hardly need point out that these emotions become further interrelated with other primary and learned emotive patterns as they help to define what it means to exist and survive as a person. Indeed, it is not careless, figurative expression that leads persons to speak of "the hunger and thirst after righteousness," the "re-creation," the "peace," the "rest" afforded in aesthetic and religious experience. For such "motifs" in the life of the person are hardly "sheer accretions" but rather special phases of a total search for quality that may well spring from these and other primary emotions.

Notes for Chapter Eight

1. There has been considerable discussion recently of the
    relation of "object" to emotion and feeling. Are
    feelings and emotions contingently related to an object?
    Should the object of an emotion, for example, be
    distinguished from its cause? I have been indicating my
    view, but more discussion is needed. Especially
    pertinent to the discussion of Freud's views, is David
    Sachs' "On Freud's Doctrine of Emotions," in Freud: A
    Collection of Critical Essays, ed. Richard Wollheim (New
    York: Doubleday, 1974).

2. Ruth and Edward Brecher, An Analysis of Human Sexual
    Response (New York: Little Brown, 1966), xiii. In an
    essay, "A Defense of Love and Morality," McCall's
    (November, 1966), Masters and Johnson themselves
    distinguish sex, as essentially a biological
    reproductive drive, from "sexuality," (p. 102), a
    "quality of living as a sexually motivated being [that]
    does not suddenly emerge at puberty...is not born of
    glandular change and the ability to reproduce" (p.
    103).

3. As James Hillman notes: "The term `libido' is a complex
    image which Freud's genius struck upon to bring together

a group of ideas which were already contained, so to speak, in the word itself. In the Roman god, _Liber_, we have the notion of a procreative, phallic principle. In _libet_, _lubet_ (_libens_, _lubens_) we have the notion of pleasure. Libido as a flow of energy is found in the Latin root, _libare_--to pour liquid." _Emotion_ (London: Routledge and Kegan Paul, rev. ed., 1962), 76, footnote; borrowing from R.B. Onians, _The Origins of European Thought about the Body and Mind, the Soul, the World, Time and Fate_ (Cambridge: Cambridge University Press, 2d. ed., 1954), 472-473. Fertility, the flow of life as yielding pleasure, freedom, creativity, all were caught up in "_libido_."

4. Ruth and Edward Brecher, ibid., xiii, xiv.

5. Irving Singer, _The Goals of Human Sexuality_ (New York: Norton, 1973).

6. See my book, _Sex, Love, and the Person_ (Mission, Kansas: Andrews and McMeel, 1967), and my article, "The Search for Meaning in Adolescent Sexuality and Love," _Teachers College Record_, 80 (3, February, 1979:483-507).

7. William McDougall, _Energies of Men_ (New York: Scribner's Sons, 1933), 99.

8. I argue that these larger valuative and qualitative ramifications of sex are critical for a more meaningful, personal, sexual experience in _Sex, Love, and the Person_ (Mission, Kansas: Andrews and McMeel, 1967). See also

Rollo May, <u>Love and Will</u> (New York: Norton and Co., 1969).

9. McDougall, ibid., 119.

10. McDougall, ibid., 98.

11. Drever seems to add sex as an appetite, along with "primary disgust" and "personal isolation." See <u>The Instinct in Man</u> (Cambridge: Cambridge University Press, 1917), 249.

12. Magda Arnold, <u>Emotion and Personality</u>, vol. 2, 174, italics added. See her comprehensive review of the physiological action patterns involved in hunger-eating phenomena.

13. Arnold, ibid., 180.

14. Arnold, ibid., 171.

15. Arnold, ibid., 177, italics added.

16. James Ward, <u>Psychological Principles</u>, 2d. ed. (Cambridge: Cambridge University Press, 1920), 2.

CHAPTER NINE

Primary Emotions: Anger, Fear, and Tenderness

In presenting primary emotions as different as hunger, lust-sex, and respect-deference, I have focussed on the experienced quality and the situational object-meaning to distinguish each tendency. This does not mean that in the total life of a person, at different stages of development, the nature of the involvement of physiological and behavioral factors does not need careful attention if we are to understand the dynamics of each primary emotion.[1] This will be evident as we consider other primary emotions.

I have resisted the temptation to think of human forms of existence and development as analogous to those which appear in subhuman species. An animal is not a dehumanized being; a person is not an animal with accretions added in the evolutionary process. It may well be, I have argued throughout, that "origins" are better understood when "the higher" is not seen simply as a "development" of "the lower." Nowhere are these cautions more relevant than in the study of fear and anger.

A. Controversy about anger, fear, and aggression.

1. Konrad Lorenz has called anger and fear, along with hunger and sex, the "constructors of evolution." On this view, the aggressive behavior that so often springs from these motives sets fundamental problems for theory about the foundations of social institutions. The controversy evoked by this and similar instinctivist views is worth noting.

Ashley Montagu is plainly irate in his preface to Man and Aggression[1], a book in which the works of Konrad Lorenz are subjected to review by able critics. Montagu himself is convinced that L.L. Bernard's Instinct: A Study of Social Psychology[2] has once and for all shown that the existence of instincts in man "has no scientific validity whatever."[3] I must wonder how carefully Montagu has examined the kinds of refinements of instinct theory to be found in the works, for example, of McDougall, J. Drever, R. Fletcher, N. Tinbergen,[4] and A. Maslow.[5] Alongside Montagu's more scientific objections there is no mistaking the social convictions that ground his animus. He is adamant against innate motives that would encourage any doctrine of original sin or depravity to which persons can resort to explain their violent behavior.

However, many anti-instinctivists have seemed to be entirely insensitive to what is at stake when they, rejecting innate motives, substitute an omnibus "urge to survival" that never accounts for the admitted qualitative discontinuities in the meaning of "survival." At critical points, they chant "transformation" when what is required is confrontation of the fact that, granted the plasticity of human motivation and behavior, qualities of motivation appear that bear no resemblance to the "sheer survival" motive from which the learned motives are presumably derived. It will hardly do, in short, to object to the reification of instinct and then appeal, at critical points, to an omnibus "will to live" to explain why certain distinctive motives are developed.

2. But some instinctivists use the same faulty mode of explaining new motives (and emotions) that have apparent continuity with their supposed origins. Thus Konrad Lorenz slides back and forth from aggression, as the survival-motive, to aggression as the main servant of survival. Moreover, aggression itself becomes another blanket-concept. Lorenz, recognizing different motives--like anger, sympathy, sex, mastery, and tenderness--subsumes them under the survival -motive, or under aggression-for-survival. Like Montagu, he seems unaware of the alchemy involved when he derives such qualitatively different motives from the

omnibus motive, survival.

The controlling fact, I must again press, is that we begin not with "life," not with an omnivorous "urge to survive," but with the actual qualities and forms of motivation that characterize us as persons. And this means that from the beginning we should take into account the kinds of wanting-knowing sensitivity unique to persons.

3. Accordingly, as I turn to an examination of anger-pugnacity and fear-escape in persons, I bear in mind: Be not surprised to find qualitative and quantitative differences in the means and ends of human e-motivation, because, at the human level, distinctive physiological and mental abilities make themselves felt. We cannot assemble persons from "simpler" elements, or assume that the emotive-hedonic responses we find in persons are miraculous extensions and transformations of "basic analogues" in animals. At the same time, we need to take note both of each distinctive, complex tendency as it appears and matures, and of its particular relation to other innate and acquired motives.

It is noteworthy that while persons experience anger and fear (each with its own meaning-object and objective), the evoking of each occurs in relation to other motives and ongoing processes. I can understand the reason for not wishing to assert that "anger" and "fear" are experienced as such by the immature human infant whose motivational tendencies are indeed restricted. For example, Montagu (despite his non-instinctivist avowals) says: "The fact is that, with the exception of the instinctoid reactions in infants to _sudden_ withdrawals of support and to sudden loud noises, the human being is entirely instinctless."[6] I would nevertheless focus on the neglected fact that "sudden" presupposes meaning-response. What is "sudden" withdrawal of support or "sudden" loud noise differs within the life of the maturing infant. "Sudden" presupposes a context of meaning, and we do well to follow what is "sudden" in an individual's context to understand his fear. In any case, we should hardly expect a well-differentiated emotive predisposition in a person with limited cognitive development. As the infant's capacity for cognitive differentiation develops, predispositional tendencies may be expected to mature. Thus, in this instance, as the context of meaning develops, a more distinct "fear-escape" tendency may well be expected.

The same thesis, that predispositions are experienced in total meaning-contexts in the lives of persons, is evident once we observe that anger is experienced not only "for itself" but in the context of other ongoing concerns. As McDougall says, anger "stands in a peculiarly intimate relation with every other one [propensity]." For anger "is called into play by thwarting or obstruction of any other active tendency....In man, with his greater range of insight and foresight, the energy of the anger-impulse may combine in very subtle ways with all other tendencies to reinforce and sustain them."[7]

I have been purposely referring to what even non-instinctivists are likely to regard as innate tendencies --despite differences in nomenclature--to justify my stress on distinguishing the meaning-pole involved at any stage in a person's life, and not the forms of behavior alone. With this background, I add three primary emotive tendencies to those proposed already.

B.   The primary emotion: anger-pugnacity

1. Anger-pugnacity is the emotion exerienced when any situation is perceived as obstructing the gratification of some want or process deemed important by the person. The objective is to remove the obstruction. The situation, of course, need not be perceptual; the human being can become angry when imaginary and conceptual situations are deemed obstructive to what he wants.[8] I am using, here and elsewhere, the word perceive broadly; it should be understood that a person's cognitive process extends from the relatively uninterpreted given pole of sensory experiences through perceptual and conceptual interpretations and constructions. Hence the same situation that arouses anger, reinterpreted, can elicit fear, or wonder, or creativity. As long as the agent interprets the situation as an impediment, he experiences anger and

"fights" his obstacle. His anger "gives way" as the obstacle is overcome, or as the situation is reinterpreted and other responses become regnant.

2. It is not unusual for scholars to substitute the language of behavior for anger-pugnacity. They then talk of aggressive and hostile behavior, or "aggression," and subsume human and subhuman responses under the same term. Whatever the language used, the text still invariably reveals--as does Lorenz's On Aggression--that, by analogy with human experience, aggression (or anger) is said to take place when the situation involves interference with some prior, or contemporary, telic action. All the more important it becomes not to neglect the fact that, at the human level, behavior that is called "aggressive" or "hostile" may stem from anger, from fear, from tenderness, from lust, or other emotions. Indeed, what one realizes vividly, as he reads Lorenz's analysis of animal behavior, is that there are many ways of dealing with obstacles, and that any particular way taken depends on the total meaning for the animal. All the more do I press my thesis that behavior at the human level is never an adequate index to the motive or emotion.

The following passage from McDougall, though it has much in common with Lorenz's discussion of aggression, does not fail to bring out the difference made by meaning to the agent. "Many a little boy has, without example or suggestion, suddenly taken to running with open mouth to bite the person who angered him, much to the distress of his parents. As the child grows up, as self-control becomes stronger, the life of ideas richer, and the means we take to overcome obstructions to our efforts more refined and complex, this instinct ceases to express itself in its crude natural manner...; the energy of its impulse adds itself to and reinforces that of other impulses and so helps us to overcome our difficulties."[9] It is interesting to note that Isidor Chein distinguishes behavior by the fact that it is action directed as well as spontaneous. "Behavior is any spontaneous directed action."[10] In sum, it is the person, capable of interpreting situations, who fears, or becomes angry, because he is unable to reinterpret that situation; or, having reinterpreted it, he is unable to control his total being to respond in accordance with his approved goal. The consequences of an emotion may be suppressed, but the supplanting of the emotion by another does not take place as long as the situation is interpreted in the same way.

All of which takes us back to a central thesis: the fact that anger-pugnacity involves certain physiological changes, that certain modes of behavioral response are modifiable, should not dilute the nuclear importance of its own meaning -object and objective as directive, if not all-controlling. An angry person may fight against the perceived or conceived obstacles by defusing them through reinterpreting the situation, or he may proceed to act in the symbolic way of baring his teeth, or by destroying his "enemy" by lies. But we block the way to adequate appreciation of varied, human angry-behavior if we neglect the context of meaning for the agent.

C.   The primary emotion: fear-escape

1. Fear-escape is the primary emotion a person experiences when something in his situation is perceived as threatening him in some way. If the obstruction to a desired objective is not interpreted as threatening, the person may experience anger; but anger gives way to fear-escape when the obstruction is interpreted as threatening. The degree of fear, the means of escape taken, will differ according to the evaluation of the threat, and of course, on whether fear dominates the situation or shares it with other emotive thrusts.

Accordingly, the less acute the interpretive awareness of a person (as, for example, in childhood or old age), the more likely is the person to over-evaluate or under-evaluate his situation as threatening. A person takes whatever action he believes at the time will reduce the perceived threat in that situation. Sheer bewilderment may take place in a situation so confusing to the experient that he is unable to focus either thought or behavior. The horror experienced by a terrified person is never to be minimized. The "suddenness" of events, actual or in prospect, may threaten human capacity to cope. But caution could be defined as fear with its eyes open.

2. So many objectively oriented studies have neglected the fact that this primary emotion cannot be abstracted from the situation as perceived by the experient. The "stimulus" is then talked of in "objective" terms--that is, as the situation appears to the observers. But it is the relationship as the interpreting-interacting person sees it that is important; the response depends on how far the person feels capable of dealing with the predicament as envisioned. Thus, as every teacher knows, his own attempt to challenge a student to take a growth-step may be taken as a threat by the student whose main aim is to "get by."

3. Generalizing, the inciting "stimulus," be it in childhood, in adolescence, or adulthood, is what comes into a life as something "sudden" in the sense that the person knows no way in which he may cope with it; the "stimulus" as perceived or conceived is what evokes the emotive response. Spinoza put it well: "...I saw that all the things I feared and which feared me had nothing good or bad in them save insofar as the mind was affected by them..."[11]

4. In sum, the total person, at his stage of development, is engaged "actively-passively" in his emotive dispositions. Hence, what begins as predispositional fear-escape, with its usually dominant, physiological, and behavioral responses, may yield to, or fuse, with anger. Or it may yield, in a reinterpretation of the situation, to wonder, or to zest and

to other emotive-complexes. When fear dominates, the situation is seen as one that could injure or destroy whatever at the moment is conceived of as being valuable.

The imaginary consequence, the danger as conceived, is always related to something prized, and the goal is avoidance of that danger. One can understand why emotions are said to be disturbing, or productive of unreasonable actions, when anger and fear are taken as exemplars in some of their expressions. Nobody who has been terrified or horrified can deny the unreasonable behavior he is at least tempted to take, or the exaggeration in imagination and thought to which he is subject. But he also knows that anger and fear can contribute much to his appreciation of himself and of so much in his total milieu.

D.   Fear, anxiety, and guilt

There is inadequate space to deal with the immense literature on anxiety--although so much of it suffers from loose definition and vagueness and "pseudo-psychotherapism." I confine myself to aspects that will help to clarify my central theme.

1. To the extent that he cannot adequately anticipate consequences in situations, and remains uncertain of consequences deemed dangerous, the person will experience anxiety. It is for this reason that a more accurate appraisal of one's situation can reduce anxiety by

clarifying the object of fear. Anxiety thrives on uncertainty in the human situation, because human beings can so readily misconstrue the actual state of affairs. Since what one fears is related to what one values, it is all the more important to realize that circumscribing the causes of anxiety be as accurate as possible.

For example, an aspect of Rollo May's otherwise excellent definition calls for further clarification. To quote: "I define anxiety as the apprehension cued off by a threat to some value the individual holds essential to his existence as a self."[12] The phrase "to his existence as a self" says too much and too little. For it may refer to biological survival, or to any value, or set of values, central to the self-concept with which the person identifies not merely his survival but his well-being. That it is well-being May stresses is clear when he says: "The understanding of anxiety can thus never be separated from ethical symbols, which are one aspect of the human being's normal milieu."[13] 2. However, we are now in an area where psychological description has passed over into ethics. May clearly is presupposing some norm when he says: "Normal anxiety is anxiety which is proportionate to the threat, does not involve repression, and can be confronted constructively on the normal level (or can be relieved if the situation is altered)."[14] Still, to remain within a more neutral context, we may say that a person experiences anxiety when he interprets (correctly or incorrectly) his specific, or total, situation in the light of facts that _for_ _him_ promise, with different degrees of uncertainty, danger to what he deems valuable. What a person suppresses, or represses, will depend on the way in which his norm, involving both conscious and unconscious factors, functions in his total value-horizon. In the same context, May concludes that "when the values [of a culture] are in disunity, the individual, feeling himself without moorings, tends to evade and repress his normal anxiety. Thus values and anxiety are closely related."[15] Hence, what is normal and what is neurotic anxiety will need to be defined not only in relation to some socially accepted norm, but also to the reconstruction of the norm a person may hold himself to.

3. The importance of being aware of the value-horizon within which both "subject" and "analyst" are making judgments about anxiety is not academic. Too many persons mouth the word anxiety as if anxiety is to be avoided at all costs. Yet, even in suggesting that persons should accept the fact that uncertainties are part of finite, changing experience, we are making a value judgment that involves a larger ethical horizon.

We remind ourselves that Plato and Aristotle would have us meet fear and anxiety with courage; the Christian would add faith and hope, while the Hindu and Buddhist focus on particular qualities of detachment. The great ethico-religious systems have been part of the human answer to the twin-problems: Which developments in personal and social styles of life cope most adequately with fear and anxiety? What values should guide us in accepting or enduring, or..., or..., fear and anxiety?

4. Much more than a passing comment should be added about conflating the experience of guilt with anxiety. I suggest that anxiety is not identical with guilt. For a person cannot deal with guilt as he deals with anxiety. If, for example, I feel anxiety, a reinterpretation of the situation may remove uncertainty, and my anxiety will be relieved. But if I have purposely chosen what I believed to be wrong, the clarification does not relieve me of guilt, and I must bear it (and perhaps do other things to reduce bad consequences).

To some readers this line of argument may seem unnecessarily cruel. But not to be aware of this difference, to conceive anxiety and guilt as identical and thus treat them alike is to inflict wounds rather than to give the treatment each deserves. Each, anxiety and guilt, tells us about different situations persons confront and of their modes of response. Each involves different modes of endurance and alleviation.

Nor is it without point, in a so-called "age of anxiety," to wonder whether too much has been laid at the door of fear and anxiety when, in fact, what is involved is guilt. Again, emotions like "remorse" and "shame" are inadequately defined, and they do defy easy definition, but are they reducible to fear and anxiety? Even more, to refer to guilt, moral disapproval, anxiety, shame, remorse as if they were all forms of fear, is like using an axe to change the contour of wood whose grain responds more adequately to different chisels.

      E.   Tenderness-protection

1. Tenderness-protection is the primary emotion experienced when a person interprets a being's situation as helpless and requiring aid. The objective is to protect that being from impending harm. (Tenderness is not to be identified with sympathy; see chapter 11.) The questions we now must ask are: Do we find ourselves emotively predisposed to be protective when we interpret a being to be helpless and needing aid? Is it reasonable to suppose that this emotion can be derived from some other, or that the emotion, as opposed to fitting protective behavior, can be learned?

Much of the problem in defining and defending this emotion as primary centers around the difficulty of characterizing what one means by "helpless." I have no doubt about the unique emotive-impetus as experienced, and of the fact that it is experienced when a being (and it may be oneself) is interpreted as helpless in the sense of being so situated that he is not able to help himself. But it is not easy to circumscribe the scope of helplessness, or how much "impending harm" it takes for the emotion to be activated--although we must also avoid thinking that an emotive response must be intense.

If the test of innateness were "present at birth," there would be no case, of course, for tenderness-protection. But what is being asserted is that when the agent comes to the point--however transient or enduring it may be--that he interprets a situation as involving helplessness, he will experience the tendency to relieve the helplessness. At the same time, every person who experiences tendernes knows that here, as elsewhere in his emotional life, he may go to the aid of the helpless against his better judgment (and of course often do the wrong thing "to help" in a particular situation). Several comments may illuminate the meaning underlying this conception of tenderness-protection.

2. This emotive response has often been the one connected with the parental, or even more specifically, with the mother instinct. It is interesting to note that Howard Warren's Dictionary of Psychology (1934) does not include a definition of the emotion tenderness. Warren does define "parental behavior" as "concern with the care and protection of the young,"[16] including both maternal and paternal behavior. At the same time, Warren defines "pity" as "an emotional attitude in which the misfortune or ills of another individual arouses a feeling of sadness or tender solicitude."[17] Thus, problems earlier mentioned concerning nomenclature face us again; but they need not obscure underlying meanings. Others may wish to use the word "pity"

rather than "tenderness," but pity seems to be a more complex emotional fusion of at least sadness and tenderness.

My suggestion here is also that the experience of tenderness, with its impulse to protect, is by no means limited to one's own offspring. To be sure, the reasons for being especially sensitive to the helplessnes of one's own children, and especially on the part of the mother, are easy to understand. What I do urge is that the root emotive experience and objective is to help or protect a being (or beings) conceived of as "helpless and needing protection" (whether or not the protection is or can be given). Protection may not be attempted if the agent believes that the helplessness and suffering is deserved, in accordance with his value-outlook.

3. Tenderness is not sympathy. In sympathy, as I shall argue later, the emotive quality is different, and the meaning-object is a being conceived to be suffering. There is, I think, no mistaking the difference in emotive quality, once we attend carefully, as we undergo tenderness and as we undergo sympathy, and once we realize that one is readily supplanted by the other, or "fuses" with the other, as meanings change. And here, surely, the behavior that expresses my emotion would not of itself readily convey to another whether it is tenderness or sympathy that I am experiencing. I can experience both tenderness and sympathy toward a suffering person; but a suffering person need not be helpless, and vice-versa. In any case, I can experience

tenderness without experiencing sympathy. Once more we realize the importance of the meaning-object in the experient's life-history and the total context he confronts. The plight of a child, of an animal, or another person facing odds beyond his power, elicits tenderness, a unique want-to-help, even if it turns out that help is not finally offered.

4. I do not concern myself here with the genetic question: When does a child begin to respond tenderly?--important as this is for the emotional education of children. My answer would take the general form, whenever the child begins to acquire his own meaning for helplessness, including his own judgment of impending harm. As we know, children can have very lively imaginations, and are prone to mistakes. Yet the fact that a child must learn what it means to be helpless does not mean that tenderness can be taught, that he learns the emotive tendency. This emotive predisposition is innately geared to this meaning; tenderness-protection is aroused to the extent tht this meaning becomes dominant in a person's experiential situation.

5. It has been wrongly assumed that if a person needs to learn a meaning, as is clearly the case with regard to "helpless", then the emotion experienced must be the product of social learning. But why should this be the case for persons who can reflect upon their experience? Why suppose that meanings are all detached or detachable from emotive predispositions? What strong evidence do we have in support

of confining cognitive meaning to interpretation independent of all emotion? Why should we not assume that as an infant grows he grows as a total being including some primary emotive responsiveness that is linked with new learned meanings? (I may remark in passing that it may be that theories of knowledge suffer insofar as they are developed without consulting what is involved in the initiation and growth of primary emotions.)

Hence, despite other uncertainties, I stand firm at one point. If we experience tenderness--and I have no doubt about it--then does it, or does it not, arise when a person becomes aware of a meaning-situation that can be articulated: "Here is a helpless being!" From what other emotive roots would this emotion be derived? As I have said, an experient may decide for any number of reasons, good or bad, that he cannot or should not help. But as long as he experiences tenderness, there is no doubting his emotive tendency, and its unique quality, in the situation as he interprets it.

This conclusion is not affectd by the fact that other persons, or other cultures, _behave_ in ways different from our own in expressing tenderness. That fact means _not_ that the emotion is learned, but only that the means of expression, different from our own, may be used to resolve the problems involved in total emotive gratification. But that means of expression are not rigidly geared to meaning -object is emphasized in the proposed theory of constitutive predispositions (thus allowing for learned dispositions within the context of meaning). Again, if we insist on holding that uniformity of behavioral response is the basic criterion for asserting the universality of a tendency or emotion, we must also be prepared to grant that, since other persons and cultures behave differently in expressing (generally admitted) universal motives such as hunger, sex, fear, and anger, these urges too are learned!

Important as behavior is to the expression of an unlearned emotion, we should expect variety of behavioral expression in the environmental learning situation as a person estimates what may be done in the situation as perceived. For example, a child out of respect (or fear or both) may help a blind person to cross the street. As he does so, he may experience tenderness, because he now realizes as never before the need of the blind for protection, and henceforth his response may be motivated both by that emotion and by respect for this blind person.

Assuming, then, that the interpretation given by the experient incites and sustains tenderness-protection, we must all the more comment that the "tenderness" that we so often appeal to, regardless of theory of emotion, can readily be overlooked as a primary motive, and this in part because no rigid or neat meaning can be given to "helpless" and "helpful." How many times every day a perceptive mother has to decide when her child is helpless and what will really help--especially if she also believes that her child must come to rely on his own ability to solve situations in which he regards himself as relatively helpless. This does not mean that she does not experience (I almost said, an even deeper quality of) tenderness, as she steels herself against offering help. It is all the more understandable that any societal code and evaluations would face, for similar reasons, some uncertainty in sorting out situations of helplessness and what ought to be done about them.

6. I have been stressing the variability in interpretations of helplessness, without giving an inch on the underived nature of the emotive disposition. My conclusion would be different if I could indicate any other emotion of which it might be an extension or from which it could be derived. At the same time, I have resisted using as a model for tenderness-protection the fascinating accounts of parental -offspring relationships in the subhuman world.

McDougall, for instance, provides an example of what may happen when a model of protective behavior, taken from the higher vertebrates, is extended to persons. He notes that for these vertebrates the protecting of their young can become, for a time at least, the all-absorbing concern of the mother--so that even fear is overcome for the sake of protecting helpless offspring. Impressed also by its value for the preservation of the species, McDougall remarks that this parental behavior is "the most powerful of the instincts."[18]

Furthermore, recognizing the anger felt when one's helpless young are threatened, McDougall sees the roots of moral indignation, justice, and public law in this alliance between parent and child. Reminding us that associative learning can take one beyond tenderness to his own child and to helpless children and animals generally, then to children and animals anyway, and finally to any adult in distress, he avers that "from this emotion and its impulse to protect... spring generosity, gratitude, love, pity, true benevolence, and altruistic conduct of every kind."[19] And James Drever concurs that it is "perhaps the only source of altruistic conduct probably more important from the social point of view than even the self-tendencies and certainly deserves the very careful attention of the moralist."[20]

7. I set aside for the moment the question of whether altruism takes root particularly in tenderness. Need I call attention once more to the umbrella-effect of explanation by the general goal of survival? In this instance, the adult experience of tenderness is interpreted phylogenetically, in terms of the role of parent in rearing the child. Human experience is seen as a "higher form" of animal experience, without asking whether that "higher" does not involve an autonomy discontinuous with any experience animals are likely to enjoy. The criterion for innateness surely should not be biased by the behavior observed at the non-human level.

For example, if a mother cat's relation to her kittens is used as an exemplar for a "maternal instinct," then it is no feat to point out that human mothers do not have the built -in capacity to seek an appropriate birthpace for their children, let alone to provide for the specific needs of the newborn. If the cat's rather elaborate, unlearned gearing of ability to motive is the criterion of a parental tendency, human mothers, who sometimes desert offspring, cannot, by comparison, be said to protect their young instinctively.

But why should we accept any animal exemplar for tendencies if we can point to the human mother's and father's protective behavior as special instances of the (broader) emotive predisposition, tenderness-protection? Why not think of a mother's tender attachment to her infant and child as a special instance of tenderness to a being usually closely linked to many values in her own life? It would be silly to minimize the power of tenderness in the life of a human mother, as is evidenced by unwed and other mothers who decide to keep the child earlier unwanted. Such considerations strengthen my contention that the interpretation of the object-situation is crucial. If the mother conceives of her baby as a threat (for any number of reasons) to other values, she may be indifferent to the helplessness of the infant and take steps to rid herself of it.

By the same token, once the emphasis is, properly, placed on the nuclear meaning, parental tenderness need not at all be confined to one's own offspring. Some persons do not adopt children because of their conviction that they might not "care" enough for an adopted baby. At the same time, it might well be that such persons would feel even more tender toward the children they adopt--indeed, would need to be even more careful in expressing their tenderness appropriately. In order to avoid over-restriction, I have preferred to "tenderness-parental," "tenderness-protection" --for the predisposition to help any being perceived to be helpless.

8. We may now ask: Assuming that there is a predisposition of tenderness-protection, does it predispose persons toward altruistic behavior? Without entering into the complexities either of defining or of justifying "altruism," it is safe to say that tenderness, like any other emotion, does not _of itself_ solve any problem of appropriate choice. The same tenderness that leads to protection can incite to over -protection and mistreatment of oneself and others. I should be the last to contend that, as such, emotive roots of human action solve the problem of knowing what the ideal for self and others is. No human emotion is _per se_ good or bad. To assume either is to presuppose a criterion for human goodness.

Nevertheless, such emotions as tenderness do make it difficult to contend, as some thinkers have, that persons are intrinsically self-seeking, or that they are all but impervious to the needs of others. However, even these other-regarding emotions are not needles of a compass pointing to the good; they are factors in the formation of

the ideal good relevant to persons. All this is another way
of saying that although one may experience the "want to
help," the emotive ferment, tenderness, does not guarantee
the quality of life for persons. The "education" of any
primary emotion is not the creation of the emotion, whatever
part it pays in the evaluation and formation of the norm of
the good for persons. The norm of altruism is not to be
prejudiced by the examination of primary emotions as such,
at least without begging the answers to ethical issues.

9. Nevertheless, it is unfortunate, I suggest, that the
rejection of a "maternal instinct" has left a vacuum in, or
a poverty-stricken approach to, what might be called the
education of tenderness.

Let us imagine, for example, a child who has acted
inappropriately in expressing his tenderness. He is scolded
or punished for behavior that is not even considered as
possibly expressing his tenderness, however "inappropriate"
it may have been. The child may be so hurt by the scolding
that his inept way of "protecting" prompted, that, on later
occasions when he experiences tenderness, he may well resist
expressing that emotion. For he has learned that "it gets
me into nothing but trouble." In a word, both suppression
(the conscious inhibition of the response to an emotion),
and repression (the attempt to keep a troublesome emotion
from becoming a factor in consciousness), can occur in
connection with tenderness, as with other emotions. This is
hardly the place to generalize about the consequences of

suppression and repression of tenderness. But how much study could have been directed to the better education of tender emotion if it had been recognized as a demanding predisposition in its own right!

F.   Tenderness-appeal?

While my discussion now must become even more tentative, I still pose the question: Is there a predisposition in the person, who experiences helplessness and suffering, to call for protection and succour? More accurately, is there a peculiar kind of emotive appeal that persons make--whether they ought to or not, whether they ought to be aided or not--when they experience helplessness?

McDougall, taking his cue once more from protective, parental behavior in the animal world, calls attention to the fact that "the object which is the primary provocation of tender emotion is, not the child itself, but the child's expression of pain, fear, or distress of any kind, especially the cry of distress; further, that this instinctive response is provoked by the cry, not only of one's own offspring, but of any child."[21] I would emphasize, rather, the situation, noted in the broader term "distress"--not "pain" and "fear"--that evokes in the "patient" a demand for help. I am not disposed, nevertheless, to minimize the testimony of parents (especially) who testify to the difference between the "cry of appeal" and the other noises and cries that their infant will emit. Which of us can seriously hold that every sound simply acquires meaning? Here, I confess to being unable at this point to describe the experienced emotive tendency to seek "help" even as I cannot disregard the different forms that "appeal" takes.

At the same time, it is worth noting that in a day when "cries of appeal" would produce an indulgent smile in the cognoscenti, much attention is being paid to the plight of loneliness and the anxieties stemming from it. Is loneliness understandable entirely as the by-product of preservative emotions, or does it spring from the experience of rejection, from a yearning for tender and sympathetic response for one's plight? Persons of all sorts, finding that the odds against them are simply too great, cry out to "all the powers that be" for help in the business of living. We may reject "the special cry of appeal" in infancy, but we cannot miss the equivalents! Note the emphasis, in some quarters, on the actual and eventual importance of "basic trust" in infancy, and, in other quarters, on the human wish to return to the womb for comfort and security, and, in still others, on the need to find security in God.

I am tempted to say that the one thing persons cannot bear psychically is that their own needs for help should occur in a world alien and impervious to them; persons prefer hate to indifference. Some existentialists have emphasized the "ontological anxiety" that is inescapable, as stemming at once from human finitude and the intimation that finitude does not tell the whole story. To set such issues aside as "theological" may itself be an escape to what seems a safer pasture!

G.   Reflective overview

1. This chapter has concentrated on human dimensions in anger-pugnacity, fear-escape, and tenderness-protection. I have further expressed my concern that even the so-called "great constructors of evolution" (to borrow Lorenz's phrase), hunger, sex, fear, and anger, must be inspected and defined at the personal level, if we are to be sensitive to different dimensions of "human survival." As I add respect and tenderness to these great constructors, I become more skeptical about reducing these primary emotions to derivatives of fear, anger, and lust, in the interest of something we call "survival" or "pleasure." I would further argue that we cannot refer either to "sublimation" as the means of moving to "higher" emotive levels from "lower" (for "sublimation" attaches a label, confidently, but without explanation), or to "transformation" of one emotion to another. How indeed can one emotion become another? Before we move along such tracks we might ask whether we can affirm that one meaning literally becomes another!

2. Psychologists of more than one school are emphasizing

that if a person is to grow he needs "to be loved"--whether he deserves it or not! At this juncture psychology joins worldviews, philosophical and theological, that concern themselves with the human need to be "saved" for a survival that is more than sheer existence. The primary emotions now to be examined define further what the quality of human survival involves.

But, as we make our transition, we remind ourselves again that we are dealing with activity-potentials in the total life of a person. The person, through maturation and learning, is always discovering what he can become; he is appraising himself in the light of actual and perceptual -imaginal-conceptual situations that also reflect the actual and interpreted appraisals of him by others in a given society. That acute observer, Lois B. Murphy,[22] warns us that rigidity of methodology will encourage neglect of the crucial fact: from the very beginning, persons must be seen as individual, developing wholes--cognitive, physiological, affective, emotive, temperamental--individual wholes, responding to themselves as well as to the environment at each "stage" in their development.

Notes for Chapter Nine

1. This view is consistent with Robert W. Leeper's conclusion: "...it really would make a great deal of difference in psychological theory if we came to think of emotions, not as primarily descriptive processes and not as primarily visceral or subcortical processes, but as main motivating processes that have the detailed, complex character that we have learned to infer from work on other perceptual or representational processes." "Some Needed Developments in the Motivational Theory of Emotions," ed. D. Levine, Nebraska Symposium on Motivation (Lincoln, Nebraska: University of Nebraska Press, 1965), 116. See also his "The Motivational Theory of Emotion," in Understanding Human Motivation, 2d ed. [eds. C.L. Stacy and M.F. Martino, (Cleveland: Howard Allen, 1963), 657-666].

2. Ashley Montagu, ed. Man and Aggression (New York: Oxford University Press, 1968). See also M.K. Wilson, ed. On Aggression (New York: Oxford University Press, 1968) and Robert Ardrey, African Genesis (New York: Athenaeum, 1961), and The Territorial Imperative (New York: Athenaeum, 1961).

3. Montagu, ibid., x. See also Montagu's more thorough statement, The Nature of Human Aggression (New York:

Oxford Press, 1976).

4. See Nikolaas Tinbergen, *Study of Instinct* (Oxford: Oxford University Press, 1969).

5. Abraham Maslow, *Motivation and Personality* (New York: Harper, 1954).

6. Montagu, ibid., 11, note 2, italics added.

7. William McDougall, *Energies of Men* (New York: Scribner's Sons, 1933), 133.

8. See McDougall, *An Introduction to Social Psychology*, rev. ed. (Boston: Luce, 1926), 61f.

9. Ibid., 63, 64, italics added.

10. Isidor Chein, *The Science of Behavior and the Image of Man* (New York: Basic Books, 1972), 77, italics added.

11. *Spinoza's Ethics* and "*De Intellectus Emendatione*," translated by A. Boyle (New York: E.P. Dutton and Co., 1910), 227.

12. Rollo May, *Psychology and the Human Dilemma* (New York: Van Nostrand, 1966), 72. See his study, *The Meaning of Anxiety*, 1950. May's book, *Love and Will*, is one of the best treatments of the dynamics of fear and anxiety. See also, William Sadler, *Existence and Love: A New Approach to Existential Phenomenology*, 1969.

13. May, ibid., 76.

14. Ibid., 71.

15. Ibid.

16. Howard E. Warren, ed. *Dictionary of Psychology* (Boston: Houghton Mifflin, 1934), 193.

17. Ibid., 203.

18. William McDougall, ibid., 69.

19. Ibid., 74, italics added.

20. James Drever, The Instinct in Man (Cambridge: Cambridge University Press, 1917), 195.

21 McDougall, ibid., 75.

22. See Lois B. Murphy, Psychoanalysis and Child Development, Part I and II, Bulletin of the Menninger Clinic, vols. 21, 22, September, November, 1957.

CHAPTER TEN

Primary Emotion: Zest

A.   Suggestive anticipation

In this chapter the question is: Do persons experience
the primary emotion, zest-mastery? I shall approach the
answer by indicating difficulties with concepts that
contribute to my view. My reader is already familiar with
my complaint that the will to live becomes an omnibus
concept into which too many varied meanings are crammed.
Moreover, when we read the statement, "Man is governed by
the will to live," close inspection usually shows that some
quality of living is actually intended.
1. Perhaps Spinoza came closest to "neutrality" in defining
the will to live. "No one, I say, refuses food or kills
himself from a necessity of his nature, but only when forced

by external causes." Then, "restating the principle in its positive form," Spinoza says that "each thing, insofar as it is in itself, endeavors (conatur) to persevere in its being."[1] As Wolfson comments, Spinoza was here denying any innate tendency to self-destruction and affirming simply the principle of continuance in existence as opposed to self -destruction.

The instability of 'persevere in its being' as such is illustrated by Thomas Hobbes, for whom self-preservation readily becomes the individual will to power. Hobbes says: "And in the way to their end, which is principally their own conservation... [individuals] endeavor (conatur) to destroy, or subdue one another."[2]

Many evolutionists, linking the will to live to the notion of natural selection, interpreted it to mean survival of the individual or the species at the expense of competitors. Some moralists tied the will to live to the innate supremacy of the demand for pleasure. And Freud's contention that the unconscious urge to pleasure (libido or id) subordinates all else to its gratification reminds us of the "blind will" in Schopenhauer's thought.

2. This very sketchy attempt to indicate the difficulty of making the generic drive to self-preservation stand still is fascinatingly illustrated in Alfred Adler's conception of preservation. For Adler the "striving for superiority," is the controlling urge toward unity of personality. But now the specific meaning of "superiority" changes. He says:

"The impetus from minus to plus never ends. The urge from below to above never ceases."[3] As Adler's authoritative expositors, Heinz and Rowena Ansbacher, comment: "At first, above meant being a real man, power, self-esteem, security; all these goal points were expressed in terms of the individual."[4] But as Adler focussed on the normal personality, "above came to mean perfection, completion, or overcoming, goal points which are no longer fully expressed in terms of the self, but which can be applied to outside objects also."[5]

When this will to live does become will-to-live-for-x (say a great upward drive to perfection), it is not clear why the particular goal is assigned (say, when "perfection" has one meaning and not another). Kurt Goldstein, for example, holds that there is one basic drive, self-actualization: "an organism is governed by the tendency to actualize, as much as possible, its individual capacities, its 'nature' in the world."[6] But if we ask what distinguishes actualization from survival, Goldstein says: "The tendency to maintain the existent state is characteristic for sick people and is a sign of anomalous life, of decay of life. The tendency of normal life is toward activity and progress,"[7] not repetition.

3. The will to live, then, is hardly a stable concept. It does indeed serve to differentiate the realm of the living from the realm of the inorganic; and it stipulates that to be alive is also to seek to preserve oneself "from within,"

in any environment. This granted,the terms self
-preservation and self-continuance simply gasp for further
definiteness since the "self" to be preserved needs to be
defined and differentiated from other selves. This calls
for distinguishing abilities and motives, insofar as they
are constitutive factors that qualify what kind of self it
is that seeks preservation. Otherwise will to live remains
an omnibus concept that, applying to all living beings,
sheds no light on the distinction between them. My main
concern is to distinguish the primary motives constitutive
of persons without separating them from each other within
the self-identifying unity of the person. In the remainder
of this chapter I shall grope my way to a definition of
zest-mastery by indicating my difficulties with instructive
segments of the work of Konrad Lorenz and Robert W. White.

B.   The will to live, aggression, and love in
        Lorenz`s theory of motivation

1. In his work On Aggression, Lorenz, intent on laying the
foundation for his conception of emotions, stresses that the
neural processes in animals are sufficiently different from
those in human beings that in principle we cannot make "any
scientifically legitimate assertion about the subjective
experiences of animals."[8] Nevertheless, he adds:
"similarities and analogies in the nervous processes of

animals and men are sufficiently great to justify the
conclusion that higher animals do indeed have subjective
experiences which are qualitatively different but in essence
[so!] akin to our own." And he concludes that, although "we
cannot know what a gander is feeling when he stands about
displaying all symptoms of human grief on the loss of his
mate, or when he rushes at her in an ecstasy of triumph on
finding her again,"[9] we cannot help feeling that whatever he
may experience is closely akin to our own emotions in an
analogous situation.

2. There is nothing in my philosophy that forbids
attributing emotion to animals, or to pressing analogies
rooted in similarities in structures. But assuming, as I do
and as Lorenz does, that animals do not have the cognitive
capacities that human beings have, I must doubt that the
qualitative differences, subjectively, of their emotions are
essentially the same.

I need not deny "ecstasy" to a gander in order to reject
its being "in essence akin to our own." But I emphatically
question the interpretation underlying Lorenz's statement
that animals are "very emotional people with very little
intelligence."[10] For this is to disregard the
differentiation of emotion in terms of meaning, to think of
human emotion as animal emotion plus intelligence. In so
doing, as I see it, Lorenz underestimates the importance of
distinctive cognitive power in the very generation of
emotion in persons, and thus actually draws analogies that

are guided by the similarity in behavioral and neural similarity at the expense of cognitive differences.

Am I succumbing to a false "human" pride when I ask: Can a gander begin to experience the ecstacy or the agony of a human being? Hardly--when I consider the differences in cognitive capacity in man and the range of human emotions that rely on meaning for the total quality of the emotive experience. It does not weaken my resistance to be told that, given the "similar constructional units" in the non-vertebrate and the vertebrate, "no reasonable person will object to calling the organ of the Cephalopods and that of the vertebrate an eye."[11] For when we are talking about emotions it is the very meaning of the situation _for_ _the_ _percipient_ that is at issue. The predispositions of a person will differ from those of a gander presumably because his very being is, in this instance, emotive-cognitive in a way not analogous to any experience of a gander. One does not add meaning _to_ emotion, or intelligence _to_ emotion--as if, in the quaint picture sometimes provided us, we were first animals, or "basically animals," and then persons.

3. I turn directly to another theoretical issue we have met before. Lorenz allows his one fundamental motive, aggression, to become the source of what we are to suppose is its opposite--even though, presumably, it is actually "in service" to aggression. It is aggression that enables the animal to live in a natural world in which it finds "not only that which is expedient, but also everything which is

not so inexpedient as to endanger the existence of the species."[12] Again, aggression is "the fighting instinct in beast and man which is directed against members of the same species."[13]

Even if I could grant aggression as the root motive, I question that such aggression within members of a species is the root of friendship and love, or what Lorenz calls "the bond" which cements individuals together. As he sees it, within a species "aggression can certainly exist without its counterpart love, but conversely there is no love without aggression..." This "personal bond," in his view, developed when, among aggressive animals, "the cooperation of two or more individuals was necessary for a species-preserving purpose, usually brood-tending. Doubtless the personal bond, love, arose in many cases from intra-specific aggression, by way of ritualization or a redirected attack or threatening."[14]

4. What becomes crucial for Lorenz's theory of motivation is the dynamics of ritualization. Thereby a newly evolved behavorial pattern achieves a "very peculiar kind of autonomy."[15] In his words, "both instinctive and cultural rituals become independent motivations of behavior by creating new ends or goals toward which the organism strives for its own sake." Again, significantly, "it is in character of independent motivating factors that rituals transcend their original function of communication and become able to perform their equally important secondary

tasks of controlling aggression and of forming a bond between certain individuals."[16]

5. We must be aware here that such ritualization as transcends original function is a theory of transformation of motives that involves a metaphysics of change, let alone an adequate psychological theory of learning. I confine myself here to challenging an assumption, crucial to the whole conception of change in personality, that is made by Lorenz and others who hold similar views. If I am to agree with them, I am to grant, for example, that a primary motive, emotion, or drive--in this instance, aggression--can cease being itself and become its opposite. In this instance, ritualization--behavior, rooted in the motive to destroy another, or to subordinate another to one's own power--can not merely redirect or control aggression but, transcending its original aim, become a bond of affection.

Now, I can understand how the behavior initiated by aggression may be inhibited, or be controlled, or otherwise modified in ways consistent with its defining goal. But when I am told that aggression itself is so redirected that it is no longer aggression, my understanding falters. When I am told that love is present where presumably only aggression was the originative motive, I ask: Is love there because aggression has ceased, or is love a form of aggression? And then I begin to wonder what kind of love it is that is a form of aggression. Nor does Lorenz help me by using a term like love, in omnibus fashion, to include even disguised hate.

6. A related problem is involved in any theory of redirection of motives that allows for their transformation (be it by ritualization or not). If redirection can transform a motive, then presumably any motive may become another. How then does one decide which motive is fundamental or originative? For example, are we ready to say that fear could become anger, or vice-versa, or that either could become sex? Such a conclusion is unacceptable to Lorenz, for example, who, as we have seen, needs some base from which to derive "higher" motives.

C. Zest-mastery as a primary emotion

1. It is in the context of such issues that I propose zest-mastery as an irreducible primary emotion. Its definition, elusive at best, may be more distinct as I relate and contrast it with Robert White's proposal of the competence motive. In using the word zest I realize that I may be doing injustice to the usual meaning of zest. I am not following the dictionary-cue that "zest" adds flavor or piquancy or enjoyment to what might otherwise become monotonous. The term zest-mastery came to me as I reflected on Charles Sherrington's phrase "zest for life" in his most stimulating book, Man On His Nature (1940).

Zest-mastery is the emotive tendency that a person experiences in a situation perceived as challenging his capacity to gain control or ascendance. It is important to recall that any situation may take on more than one meaning and evoke more than one emotion. Thus, zest-mastery may take over a situation that at first engaged some other primary emotion, such as fear, or wonder, or anger, or lust, or an acquired sentiment or attitude. Zest is not evoked until the objective is mastery of the problem simply because it is a challenge to one's own capability.

2. To be sure, anger-pugnacity may follow when zest-mastery is frustrated; or, if the situation is seen as threatening or dangerous, fear-escape may take over. But what I have particularly in mind is the grip that a situation has when it challenges a person's efficacy, his capacity to master the problem that means _for_ _him_, "acting myself," in relation to it. Zest galvanizes the person to get on with the mastering of a task as so conceived, self-assigned or otherwise. The _result_ is a new awareness of what his being counts for in that situation. However, this is not to say that _the_ aim is "self-discovery," which too readily becomes another omnibus-label.

3. Finally, zest-mastery does not solve the problem whether man is basically egoistic or altruistic. For, plainly, one feels zest as he masters obstacles involved in sharing, or in enslaving. Zest-mastery must not be confined to any one evaluation of mastery. A.N. Whitehead's words are congenial to me here: "At the base of our existence is the sense of 'worth'....Here the notion of worth is not to be construed

in a purely eulogistic sense. It is the sense of existence for its own sake, of existence which is its own justification, of existence with its own character."[17] What I wish to emphasize is 'its own character,' the assertion of one's being whatever one can be, or thinks he can become. It is the elusive, yet more specific, positive _quality_ of "worth" that I am trying to capture by "zest"--within the total emotive matrix of the person. It is not something normative, such as is hidden in most talk about "self -actualization" or about being "authentic."

D.   Robert White's conception of the competence motive

Thus far I have rejected any primal urge that is so loosely defined that its branches can be allowed to bear many fruits and its energies transformed miraculously into even opposing motives. At the same time, I have found it no easy task to describe the experience of zest-mastery, or to isolate its thrust clearly from other primary motives of the self-identifying person. All the more gladly do I turn to the psychology of personality developed by Robert W. White, because I find much in the competence motive he advances that confirms what I have been trying to capture in _zest-mastery_. Yet there are tensions in his conception that bring out my underlying concern.

1. Why did Robert White propose a competence motive at a time when either anti-instinctivism or some form of Freudian instinct-theory were gaining much of the attention of psychologists? Because he found it possible to unite two persistent convictions in his theory of motivation: a biological and a non-biological.[18]

His "biological view of man" emphasizes that "tissue conditions set off persistent lines of behavior....However susceptible to change through learning, the human motivational system has its roots in the simple necessities of growth, maintenance, and reproduction."[19] However, his non-biological view allows him to recognize "investigating tendencies" in man for which no bodily structures can be specified. Hence, basic motives are to be defined not solely in terms of survival-value.

The following passage introduces White's appeal to competence and the feeling of efficacy.

> The human infant is born conspicuously incompetent. He has everything to learn about his surroundings and how he can affect them. Behavior activated by drives like hunger, sex, and avoidance of pain will teach him a number of things about the environment, but it is through play, manipulation, and exploration that he rounds out his cognitive map and perfects his capacities. Human beings are often active when their drives are at rest; they reach out toward

the environment and expose themselves to it. It is therefore useful to think of exploratory and manipulative behavior as representing a form of persistent motivation, the biological function of which is to develop competence in dealing with the environment. To the extent that competence is actually achieved, it contributes to feelings of efficacy which are an important ingredient of self-esteem.[20]

This passage expresses part of White's concern that an adequate dynamic psychology must rid itself of any psychoanalytic framework that suffers from limiting itself to the study of blocked and disordered behavior; it must develop concepts more adequate to everyday "lives in progress" and to "a thorough exploration of the patient's emotional life."[21]

2. Nevertheless, White wants both to stay within the biological frame-work supported by evolutionary thought, to profit from the revolution effected by psychoanalytic ways of dealing with disordered personalities, and yet be faithful to his conviction that these approaches never quite do justice to the fact that "personality is a constantly evolving system." In any case, his appeal to the motive of competence, to the "feelings of efficacy," does in fact take him beyond a conception of growth as sheer survival-value, or of explanation by origins alone.

The conception is supported further by White's stress on the conflict between the "push" of drive and the "pull" of initiative. This conflict surfaces as he speaks of "an inherent tendency or motive toward activity, taking the form of exploration, manipulation, and playful testing of surroundings," activities that also have "the biological significance" of attaining competence in dealing with the environment. "More clearly than other concepts, this idea restores to the person what we all experience as initiative and efficacy in leading our lives."[22]

What troubles me in this passage, and others, is the emphasis on the "inherent tendency or motive toward activity" that seems to result in competence and the experience of "initiative and efficacy." Thus the "tendency toward activity" moves toward becoming an omnibus motive expressed in the forms of adaptive exploration and manipulation, and the "feelings of efficacy" tend to be accompaniments of competence rather than the actuality in the impetus to competence.

It is this quality in "feelings [emotion] of efficacy" that I would capture in zest-mastery, even as I disassociate myself from the problems I have referred to in the concept

of transformation of motives. I grant the drift, but remain
uneasy, when I read:

> A clear advantage in terms of survival would
> appear to lie with a creature that spontaneously
> explored and manipulated things, building up <u>out
> of sheer curiosity</u> a certain knowledge and skill
> in dealing with the environment; this prior
> competence might well make the difference
> between life and death in a crisis provided by
> hunger, thirst or external danger. But we need
> not rely on speculation. Observation of young
> animals and children reveals a great deal of
> playful, manipulative, and exploratory activity
> <u>that seems to go on without the instigation of</u>
> <u>visceral drives</u>. These activities are done for
> the fun of it, but they serve a serious
> biological purpose. Part of the fun can be
> described as a <u>feeling</u> <u>of</u> <u>efficacy</u>--or sense of
> mastery--and the biological purpose is clearly
> the attaining of <u>competence</u> in dealing with the
> environment.[23]

3. Can we grant the seeming assimilation of "sheer
curiosity," or "exploratory activity" to "attaining of
competence?" May a person not explore for the sake of

exploring, whether he masters or not? Moreover, can we still define man as an evolutionary creature in the usual biological sense of survival-value if we take seriously a statement like the following? "Active exploration, curiosity, play, aesthetic interests, the enjoyment of thinking, and many other characteristic human concerns take an intelligible place in the biological view of man."[24]

Yet White himself says that students of personality should not be held back by scientific, "finer discriminations" between the instinct of curiosity, the exploratory drive, the need for varied sensory stimulation, or the joy of being a cause. For they should note the common bearing of curiosity and similar finer discriminations on the development of effectiveness.[25] Thus White continues: "If in our thinking about motives we do not include this overall tendency toward active dealing we draw the picture of a creature that is helpless in the grip of its fears, drives, and passions, certainly too helpless to have been the creator of civilization."[26] Hence, White's stress falls not on survival-value but on attaining competence, on the power of initiative and exertion that animates our sense of being agents, namely, "a feeling of efficacy."

4. I submit that there is no more than a difference in words between "feeling of efficacy" and "sense of competence," and what I mean by "zest-mastery." But I wish to leave no doubt

that the emotive impulse in <u>zest-mastery</u> is not identical
with the emotive tendencies that I shall later differentiate
in <u>wonder-curiosity</u> and <u>creativity-enlivenment</u>.[27] Yet the
experience to which <u>zest</u> points is indeed the "emotion of
efficacy," or "the sense of being an agent"--"I don't want
to be a zero!"

To conclude, we shall be losing a very significant focus
of personal existence if we do not recognize zest-mastery as
a distinct primary motive, as a relatively autonomous
yearning within the active unity of the being-becoming
person. Much of the sadness, depression, and even despair
in living comes when a person does not experience situations
in which he can affirm: "I make a difference!"

     E.   Reflective overview

To will to live as a person is not only to continue, or
"preserve" one's existence. It is also to be intent on
surviving as a being animated by one among other objectives,
namely, to make a difference in terms of some competence
significant to oneself at least. It is this experience that
I seek to fence in by <u>zest-mastery</u>, without suggesting that
it involves, antecedently to learning, some specific goal.
For a person to "assert himself" is not for that person to
be self-ish. Nor does it entail any form of altruism. In
the course of "being themselves" persons have run the
gauntlet from "sacrificial" to "parasitic" living. The

<u>quality</u> of life that the person is to have will depend on what he decides is valuable to him, given the dimensions of his being as he interacts with his environments.

Notes for Chapter Ten

1. Benedictus Spinoza, Ethics, Book IV, Scholium to Proposition 20, and Proposition 6, as quoted by Harry A. Wolfson, The Philosophy of Spinoza (Cambridge: Harvard University Press, 1948), 2 vols. in 1, 198.

2. Thomas Hobbes, Leviathan, Book I, 13, as quoted by Wolfson, ibid., 197, note 1.

3. As quoted in The Individual Psychology of Alfred Adler, edited and annotated by Heinz L. and Rowena R. Ansbacher (New York: Basic Books, 1956), 103.

4. Ibid., 101.

5. Ibid., 102.

6. Kurt Goldstein, The Organism: A Holistic Approach to Biology Derived from Pathological Data in Man (New York: American Book Company, 1939), 196.

7. Ibid., 197.

8. Konrad Lorenz, On Aggression. Translated by Marjorie K. Wilson (New York: Harcourt Bantam Edition, 1966), 202.

9. Ibid., 202, 203.

10. Ibid.

11. Ibid., 211.

12. Ibid., 148.

13. Ibid., ix.

14. Ibid., 209.

15. Ibid., 74.

16. Ibid.

17. Alfred N. Whitehead, Modes of Thought (New York: Macmillan Co., 1938), 149.

18. Robert W. White, Lives in Progress: A Study of the Natural Growth of Personality (New York: Holt, Rinehart and Winston [1952] rev. ed. 1966). I shall confine myself largely to this book since White's theoretical struggle comes out here more clearly than in the more systematic The Enterprise of Living: Growth and Organization in Personality (New York: Holt, Rinehart and Winston, 1972). See also his "Competence and the Psychosexual Stages of Development" in Nebraska Symposium on Motivation (1960).

19. White, Lives, 5.

20. Ibid., 7, italics added.

21. Ibid., 11.

22 Ibid., 25, italics added.

23. Ibid., 247, 248, italics added except in the last sentence. See also White's "Motivation Reconsidered: The Concept of Competence," Psychological Review, 66 (1959): 297-335.

24. Ibid., 249. See also Enterprise (1972), 246.

25. See White, Enterprise (1972), 246.

26. White, Enterprise (1972), 209.

27. See chapter Eleven.

CHAPTER ELEVEN

Primary Emotions: Sympathy, Wonder, Creativity

A.   Sympathy-Succour

I have been distinguishing primary emotions without which
we cannot adequately envision what survival means for
persons. Three other prominent emotions--sympathy, wonder,
creativity--are generally derived from other, unlearned
tendencies. Difficulties regarding nomenclature aside, I
suspect that the failure even to consider that emotions like
sympathy, wonder, and creativity are unlearned stems in
large part from the assumption that the appearance of an
emotion at a later stage of a person's cognitive development
means that it is an acquired expression of unlearned
motives. Unhesitatingly I grant that none of these emotions
(as I shall define them) can exist in a being incapable of
the self-consciousness and the cognitive abilities that make
their appearance as a person matures beyond infancy.[1] All

along I have submitted that cognitive developments are intrinsic to unlearned emotions. In forwarding these three emotions as primary, I continue to distinguish the meaning that defines each as an irreducible qualitative tendency within the matrix of the being-becoming person.

1. Is there any predisposition that "cements" persons together, that relates them by its tendency to "care" for each other when they are conceived to be suffering? Nobody denies that persons cannot survive without each other, but the question remains: Is human togetherness and community fostered by any distinct, emotive, cooperative tendency? It is fascinating to note the length to which philosophical and psychological egoists have gone to explain the "cooperation" that persons do expect from each other to ward off danger, let alone to pursue some quality of survival.

2. Thomas Hobbes--to take a classic example--insisted on each man's innate "right" in the "state of nature" to ensure his own existence by any means. But bowing to the fact that no man has an adequate defense against death at the hands of others, Hobbes went on to argue that the only reasonable thing each man can do is to sacrifice his native right to a State that will be strong enough to protect him against the "right" of every person. This means that the "social element" that binds people together is the fear of being overpowered--no more, no less. The State thus exists to

ensure that persons take "prudent" measures against the basic tendency in their own natures. On this view, we may expect many persons, who have reluctantly given up "natural" rights, to reason: Whenever I find that I may be able to get what I want by evading the power of the State, why not turn the situation to my advantage?

Other scholars, aware of the psycho-logic of this view of individuals and society, and convinced that it could not explain the strong ties human beings do experience to each other, looked for native other-regarding tendencies in persons. They argued that the State is more than a collection of persons living ultimately in fear of each other. Ethicists and psychologists who could not find the foundations of altruism in reason, in God, or in a non-emotive moral imperative, accordingly turned to emotions like sympathy, pity, and compassion for the springs of altruism.

John Stuart Mill, for example, insisted that the ethical standard, the greatest happiness of the greatest number, is based on a "powerful natural sentiment...the social feelings of mankind; the desire to be in unity with our fellow creatures which is already a powerful principle in human nature..."[2]

3. I suggest once more that none of the primary emotions can itself provide the ground for either altruism or egotism. Apart from the difficulty of adequately defining egotism and altruism, nothing in any primary emotion itself is immune

from self-service at the expense of other persons. We must
accordingly beware of counter-posing predispositions to each
other as, for example, does Adam Smith in the opening
sentence of Theory of Moral Sentiments (1759): "However
selfish soever man may be supposed, there are evidently some
principles in his nature which interest him in the fortune
of others, and render their happiness necessary to him."[3]
Thinkers no less notable than Hume and Schopenhauer, let
alone Rousseau, have proposed non-rational tendencies, like
sympathy and pity, as the springs of altruism. Before
proposing sympathy-succour as a primary emotion, and
relating it to altruism, I shall examine briefly William
McDougall's view of sympathy.

4. Part of the problem we face in characterizing sympathy is
illustrated by McDougall's approach to it. He sees the
gregarious instinct at work in the simplest form when
animals and persons flock together, in their "mere
uneasiness in isolation and satisfaction in being one of a
herd."[4] At this stage, "the affective aspect of the
operation of this instinct is not sufficiently intense or
specific to have been given a name."[5] Consequently,
McDougall does not consider sympathy the accompaniment of a
gregarious instinct. Rather does he reserve "sympathy" for
a special kind of sensitive response by members of a
gregarious species to the emotional excitement of each
other. In his words: "The fundamental and primitive form of

sympathy is exactly what the word implies, a suffering with, the experiencing of any feeling or emotion when and because we observe in other persons or creatures the expression of that feeling or emotion."[6] Moreover, this "sympathetic induction of emotion and feeling," McDougall notes, is especially noticeable in the immediate, sensitive response of children to wailing, to smiles, and to expression of fear and anger. Among adults also, "a merry face makes me feel brighter; a melancholy face may cast a gloom over a cheerful company; when we witness the painful emotion of others, we experience sympathetic pain."[7] McDougall concludes that such primitive passive sympathy is "a special adaptation of the receptive side of each of the principal instinctive dispositions, an adaptation that renders each instinct capable of being excited on the perception of the bodily expressions of the excitement of the same instinct in other persons."[8]

5. Active sympathy is not divorced from the expression of passive sympathy for it "plays or may play a minor part in the genesis of the [learned] parental sentiment, but it is of prime importance for the development of affection among equals."[9] Reciprocal relations, sharing of emotions and similar sentiments enhance the quality of the mutual response. McDougall, again, is careful to emphasize that active sympathy "although it is not in itself an altruistic impulse and is not in any sense the root of altruism, it is

a most valuable adjunct to the tender emotion in the
formation of altruistic sentiments and in stimulating social
co-operation for social ends."[10] It seems clear that both
passive and active sympathy draw individuals together
although neither as such is a positive initiator of
altruism. In his later work, Energies of Man, McDougall
does attribute a "gregarious propensity" to man and defines
it as the innate tendency "to remain in company with fellows
and, if isolated, to seek that company."[11] All the more,
then, whereas tenderness is the emotion accompanying the
innate parental propensity, sympathy is not an emotion but
the receptive side of each primary propensity. Minimally,
it is a person's unlearned sensitivity, strengthened by
habit, to the emotional responses of others, and only as it
becomes attached to altruistic sentiments does it contribute
to altruism.[12]

6. I shall assume that McDougall's account of passive and
active sympathy can withstand criticism insofar as it
distinguishes qualitative levels of companionship. Yet I
miss in McDougall's discussion a quality of emotion as such
that is probably absorbed in McDougall's conception of the
parental propensity and its accompanying emotion of
tenderness. Hence I suggest that sympathy is a distinct
primary emotion experienced by a person when he conceives
another person or creature as suffering. The suffering
incites the impetus to relieve that suffering (succour).

The emphasis is not on how (involving, perhaps, passive or active sympathy) one knows that another being is suffering; it is not on actually relieving the distress of the person experiencing sympathy-succour, but on the impetus to relieve the suffering as conceived. Bishop Butler's perceptive observation is very relevant. "The sight of a man in misery," he says, "raises our compassion toward him, and, if this misery be inflicted on him by another, our indignation against the author of it. But when we are informed that the sufferer is a villain and is punished only for his treachery and cruelty, our compassion exceedingly lessens, and in many instances our indignation wholly subsides..."[13] What happens to the experience of sympathy, initiated by conceived suffering, depends upon a person's operative evaluation of suffering in the light of the ethical norm he has adopted.

7. Given this description of the dynamics of sympathy -succour, we cannot learn or teach sympathy, but we can learn and teach what situations are likely to involve suffering. To the extent that another recognizes that suffering is taking place, his predisposition will be aroused, although other factors in the total situation, including the present organization of his personality and his ethical norm, may keep him from acting out his sympathy.

It cannot be over-emphasized that much of what we, as observers, take to be suffering is not suffering to those we believe to be suffering and vice-versa. Furthermore, we are often inept in our attempts to relieve the suffering of others, because we do not appreciate the quality of suffering in the total situation as it is conceived by the "sufferers."

8. If then, we ask: If a person is aware of a meaning -situation in which suffering (not helplessness) is present, does he experience the predisposition to relieve that suffering, whether or not he finally does act to relieve it, or does so appropriately? Is it reasonable to suppose that sympathy-succour as experienced is not reducible to any other emotion, such as fear, or anger, or even tenderness? My own answer is: Once I am aware of what I regard as suffering, I experience the impetus to relieve that suffering--even if my judgment soon tells me that I had better not. Yet I still find myself wanting to relieve that suffering, even when I judge it better not to succour; and sometimes my emotion, unapproved by my reason, overcomes.

9. Finally, sympathy-succour, as such, is not the nuclear predisposition favoring a particular norm of altruism. Its presence in persons does favor the view that the social group, be it family or state, is not an artifical adjustment that insulated individuals accept grudgingly and "against the grain"--their last ditch stand to protect their own security against ingrained individualistic tendencies in others.[14]

All in all, on the view of primary emotion here advanced,
we can hold that there are non-rational factors--especially
sympathy, tenderness, and respect--that make for
spontaneous psychic ties among persons. In themselves,
however, these emotions do not guarantee the quality of any
specific social group even though they act as "cementing
factors." Indeed, they may lead to division among persons
by pitting groups against each other and destroying such
cooperation as may spring from other causes. Unfortunately,
the statement, "Man is a social animal," is too frequently
used in the honorific sense.

B.   Wonder-Curiosity

It is a sad commentary on the way methodological
assumptions influence psychological theory when appeals to
innate wonder and curiosity in persons come into greater
vogue only after the "discovery" that some animals, such as
rats, "explore" their environment even when they are not
satiated, and sometimes at the expense of other needs. How
we would know that certain movements of animals are
"exploratory" as responses to inner needs without assuming
some analogy between motive, behavior, and situations
consciously experienced by persons remains a puzzle.
1. Once more I find McDougall's description helpful.
"Curiosity...is not called into activity by objects of any

one type only, but rather by any object or situation which involves a certain feature, namely, imperfect apprehension or perception insufficiently clear to invoke any other instinct." McDougall adds that, unlike the combative instinct, which "supervenes upon" the quest of some other instinct, "curiosity is commonly displayed as a prelude to some other mode of action."[15] Moreover, if the object of curiosity must not be so novel or unusual as to excite some other instinct, it must be sufficiently similar to "objects that normally evoke some other instinct."[16] For McDougall the emotion accompanying this propensity of curiosity is wonder.

2. My reader will correctly expect me to protest the conception of the emotion accompanying the propensity. Wonder is the tendential core of the propensity defined by the meaning-situation. In any case, I wish to emphasize that we do not "wonder" because we are curious but are curious, or "explore," as we experience wonder. And, I would urge that wonder-curiosity is related to all other predispositions because the person, in pursuing the meaning-objects of other propensities, as often as not activates wonder-curiosity.

3. In considering the nature of wonder-curiosity, we must beware lest we assume a particular theory about the relation of sense to perception and reason. At least procedurally, I agree with Brand Blanshard that: "We must not construe the

world we first live in as to make escape from it
inconceivable."[17] This takes place in psychology when we
assume that the infant and child are confronted only with
confusion. Fearing lest we impute too much to the child, we
often assert that "of course" the infant and child begin
with sensory-perceptual experience that is free of any iota
of reasoning.

Whether logical and reasoning activity are involved in
human experience, especially at any point where experiences
are connected with each other by more than sheer memory,
must be left open in this study. Any answer must, however,
comprehend the dynamic in wonder. This primary emotion is
not a specific cognitive capacity involved in knowing what
the world is. Rather does it predispose the person to know
the world (whatever that process entails). Thus, following
McDougall, I suggest that curiosity is incited by any
situation in which, for the experient at that point, there
are factors sufficiently similar and different to "release"
the predisposition to wonder. The "releaser" or "object"
need not, for persons, be sensory-perceptual, since persons
are significantly involved with conceptual problems as well.
The theme I would re-emphasize here is that the agent
experiences a distinct kind of thrust in such situations
which is not gratified until the situation becomes
sufficiently "clear" to him. "Thinking" stirred by wonder,
"exploring" activated by and sustained in wonder, has its

emotional thrust in the life of a person (whatever final
decision we come to about the cognitive processes).

4. As usual, I find in the inimitable William James an
emphasis too often neglected when we talk about reason or
reasoning. His essay, "The Sentiment of Rationality,"[18]
expresses an instrumentalist view of thought that, though
inadequate by itself, yet captures the emotive press that
one experiences when he is puzzled in a situation. James
speaks of the passion persons experience when the smooth
course of thought is interrupted or inhibited by the sheer
many-ness of things, by blurred outlines, and vague
identifications.

In such situations persons experience both the demand to
reduce "manifoldness to simplicity" and the demand to
distinguish parts within wholes. We need not confine wonder
to any specific goal; James, himself, though speaking of the
"passion for parsimony," does not restrict himself to that.
We may leave the objective, the "demands of expectancy to be
satisfied," to further definition, because the "mental
uneasiness if not distress"[19] may be relieved by different
forms of clarity (as James' own essay shows). What needs
emphasis is not only that the person experiencing wonder
will seek for whatever will reduce his puzzlement in that
situation, but also that his whole theoretic life is not an
unemotional or "cold" enterprise. At the same time, wonder-
curiosity need not be a roaring demand, but an emotive
thrust that activates the person, both as leisure and

cognitive ability and training enhance opportunity.

To summarize: part of what it means to be a person--to survive as a person--is to wonder, and the objective may be most generally stated, I suggest, as "the finding of connections with the familiar." This primary demand for a unique kind of fulfillment persists in prosaic everyday ventures and also in so much of our more venturesome moral, aesthetic, religious, and philosophical probings.

5. Unusual examples help us to appreciate both the press of wonder and the quality of being that the gratification of wonder-curiosity yields. Helen Keller, the blind and deaf mute, was taught, by manual touch, a few simple words (like d-o-l-l). She describes learning what words really meant in her experience:

> We walked down the path to the well-house, attracted by the fragrance of the honeysuckle with which it was covered. Someone was drawing water and my teacher placed my hand under the spout. As a cool stream gushed over one hand she spelled into the other the word water, first slowly, then rapidly. I stood still, my whole attention fixed upon the motions of her fingers. Suddenly I felt a misty consciousness as of something forgotten--a thrill of returning

thought; and somehow the mystery of language was
revealed to me. I knew then that 'w-a-t-e-r'
meant the wonderful cool something that was
flowing over my hand. The living world awakened
my soul, gave it light, joy, set it free! I
left the well-house eager to learn. Everything
had a name, and each name gave birth to a new
thought. As we returned to the house each
object that I touched seemed to quiver with life.[20]

6. This activity-potential, wonder-curiosity, reveals to us
once more that a person is never simply responding to a
world; he is transforming his environment from "something
impinging" into a world alive with meaning for the sake of
meaning; old, yet new; strange, yet familiar. He is struck
by the unfamiliar; he stands in awe of the "mystery of
being" perhaps, but for him as a person that mystery remains
an everlasting challenge.

In the following quotation, Alfred North Whitehead,
stressing the cognitive thrust in curiosity, at the same
time introduces a factor that allies it with what I shall
prefer to distinguish as creativity-enlivenment. His words
will mark our transition to this primary emotion. "But the
word 'curiosity' somewhat trivializes that inward motive
that has driven men. In the greater sense (in which it
characterizes science and philosophy)...curiosity means the
craving of reason that the facts discriminated in experience
be understood. It means the refusal to be satisfied with
the bare welter of fact, or even with the bare habit of
routine."[21]

C.   Creativity-Enlivenment

1. In view of the definitions of zest-mastery and of
wonder-curiosity that I have suggested, it may seem a tour
de force to propose that there is an irreducible emotion of
the person that we may call "creativity." I am somewhat,
but not altogether, arbitrarily choosing the word
`creativity' for the emotive urge experienced as the person
seeks novelty. A peculiar dullness and boredom characterize
any life without creativity. Creativity as such is never
change as change, nor competence as competence, nor wonder
as wonder; but creativity may involve each, and be a factor
in the development of other predispositions. I can find no
better word than `enlivenment' to characterize the situation
in which creativity is experienced and expressed.
2. But why introduce another primary emotion when the
others already mentioned can account for the facts? Anger,
we said, is concerned with removing an obstruction to any
wanted goal; wonder focusses the person on strange-familiar;
and zest comes into play when a person demands "to make my
own difference." Surely, creativity is the variation of any
of these, or a fusion of them?

Before answering, I take note of a relevant passage from
Hans Haas, The Human Animal, that illustrates the difficulty
of pin-pointing distinctions between emotions: "Curiosity

and play are certainly not identical in our linguistic
usage, yet it is highly probable that both phenomena have a
common root. The difference lies merely in the fact that
curiosity leads to exploration and mastery of one's
environment, whereas play leads to exploration and mastery
of new capabilities. In the first instance the prime object
is information; in the second the construction of motor
patterns. There is, however, a similar instinctive striving
for novelty in both instances."[22]

However, I find myself still asking: Are both curiosity
and mastery rooted in the "instinctive striving for
novelty?" If overt behavior alone were to be our criterion
for primary emotion, I might agree with Haas. But is his
claim acceptable if one defines zest-mastery and wonder-
curiosity from within, and distinguishes between emotive
impetus in the meaning-situation and the behavioral
response? I discern a distinct difference when the emotion,
creativity-enlivenment, is the dominant thrust toward
novelty. In short, I experience creativity-enlivenment when
I strike out in a new, not merely different, direction.
Because puzzlement may also be present, I may be
experiencing wonder at the same time, but when I experience
creativity, my concern is not to increase the familiar at
the "prompting" of the strange, but to produce some novelty
that I believe is within the scope of my abilities.
3. Perhaps, then the following words will capture the
elusive primary emotion that I forward as irreducible,

despite the temptation to derive it from close neighbors and
from other predispositions in whose expression it plays so
large a part. <u>Creativity-enlivenment is the tendency</u>
<u>experienced whenever what is conceived as novelty is deemed</u>
<u>to be within the scope of one's varied activity-potentials</u>
<u>as they are expressed and adapted in situations grown</u>
<u>familiar but uninteresting in the experient's outlook.</u>
4. From the nature of the case, I cannot stipulate any
objective situation that is bound to evoke creativity. Each
instance involves contrast with something that is conceived
as no longer novel. An emotive thrust that makes its own
demand in every dimension of life, creativity surfaces as a
refusal to endure either routine or change as such. As Lois
Murphy[23] emphasizes, while the word 'creativity' has an
honorific connotation, we must not suppose that all changes
that seem good are in fact good for the agent or anyone else
affected.

After all, we are not talking about "planned" or
"reflective" creativity, but about an e-motion needing
evaluation within any definition of the good for persons.
Of all the emotive activity-potentials, creativity-
enlivenment is the <u>tendency</u>, the want to make a <u>new</u>
difference, not just a difference. Creativity may well be a
disturber of "peace" and "harmony." Indeed, it cannot but
result in insecurity, for it introduces new tension(s) as it
thrusts us toward what may actually be within reach.

5. At the same time, I would resist the temptation to which, as I see it, Jung was victim. He hypothesized that there is one primal urge to creativity from which all other motives are derived. I have faulted as omnibus thinking the appeal to a primal "will to survive," "will to power," or a hedonistic "id." Yet, were I to hold any such primal striving, it would be creativity-enlivenment. I would, accordingly, agree with the many thinkers who see in the Promethean, in the Dionysian--not merely in the person as "maker" but in person as "creator"--the key to greatness and to folly. Persons live "on the brink" because they are never gratified or satisfied, since every gratification and satisfaction can become uninteresting, boring, and "dead." Rooted in the person's creativity-enlightenment, it is vive la difference that counts.

D.   Reflective overview

In selecting the primary emotions that are the unlearned motives of persons I have been guided by certain qualities of conscious experience that are differentiated as the tendency-goal-meaning is distinguished. This does not mean that the primary emotions are isolated from each other; their relationships need specific study in their ongoing maturation and accommodation within the individual person's being-becoming. They live, let us not forget, in the

crucible of activity-potentials that are the essence of the
self-identifying person. The part they play in the person's
own self-estimate as he interacts with his environment is
itself in the making.

I have suggested no priority among primary emotions since
that presupposes a standard for the person's development
that should not be taken for granted. Important as a theory
of emotions is to reflection on the life good to live for
persons, and important as it is to describe adequately the
nature and scope of the primary emotions, the task remains
to allow the person, part and whole, to be present in the
decisions about the good. My analysis of feelings and
primary emotions undermines some ethical systems founded
upon or heavily dependent on a faulty conception of their
dynamics. Since the essential nature of the person includes
qualitatively variable primary emotions, none of which is
geared to, or locked into, a fixed pattern of expression, no
one system of ethics is dictated by his nature. But in
closing, I suggest that the qualities of survival that
depends on the responsive-responsible cooperation of persons
does have enduring roots at least in the proposed primary
emotions.

Notes for Chapter Eleven

1. Lois B. Murphy, Personality in Young Children, vol. 2 (New York: Basic Books, 1954), chapter 17.

2. J.S. Mill, Utilitarianism (1863), ed. Oskar Piest (New York: Bobbs-Merrill, 1948), 33. See also I.D. Suttie, The Origins of Love and Hate, 1935, and M.F. Ashley - Montagu, On Being Human, 1950; P.A. Sorokin, Altruistic Love, 1950.

3. From G.W. Allport, "The Historical Background of Modern Social Psychology," in The Handbook of Social Psychology, ed. G. Lindzey and E. Aronson (Reading, Mass.: Addison-Wesley, 1968), 2d ed., 24.

4. William McDougall, Social Psychology, rev. ed. (Boston: Luce and Co., 1926), 87.

5. Ibid., 86, 87.

6. Ibid., 95, italics added.

7. Ibid., 97, 98.

8. Ibid., 98.

9. Ibid., 173; see 175, 176.

10. Ibid., 178; see 177.

11. McDougall, The Energies of Men (New York: Scribner's Sons, 1932), 97.

12. Space does not allow a comparison of this treatment with Max Scheler's in The Nature of Sympathy, ed. Peter Heath (New Haven: Yale University Press, 1954).

13. Joseph Butler, A Dissertation Upon the Nature of Virtue in Five Sermons, ed. Stuart M. Brown (New York: Liberal Arts Press, 1950), 84.

14. Philip Mercer, Sympathy and Ethics (Oxford: Oxford University Press, 1972), and Bernard Williams, Morality, An Introduction to Ethics (New York: Harper and Row, 1972), for perceptive discussion of the relation of sympathy to morality.

15. William McDougall, Outline of Psychology (New York: Scribner's Sons, 1923), 143.

16. Ibid.

17. Brand Blanshard, The Nature of Thought, 2 vols. (London: Allen and Unwin, 1939, 1948), vol. 1, 57.

18. William James The Will to Believe and Other Essays (New York: Longmans, Green, 1896; 1931).

19. Ibid., 65f.

20. Helen Keller, The Story of My Life, 1902. I owe this reference to A. Koestler, The Act of Creation (New York: Macmillan, 1964), 222.

21. Alfred N. Whitehead, Adventure of Ideas (New York: Macmillan, 1933), 180. In the same book Whitehead, speaking about reality, says: "The creativity of the world is the throbbing emotion of the past hurling itself into a new transcendent fact," 227.

320

22. Hans Haas, <u>The Human Animal</u> tr. J. Maxwell Brownjohn (New York: Putnams's Sons, 1970), p. 90; and see chapter 8.

23. Lois Murphy, <u>Personality in Young Children</u> (New York: Basic Books, 1970), 211, 212.

Index

criterion for proposed primary emotions, 211-213;

defense of qualitative differentiation, 168-171; does

not become another, 208-210; important for education,

215-218; interchangeable use with instinct, 173-175;

James-Lange theory rejected, 146-147; meaning central

to each tendency, 241-243, 299-300; and mode of

expression, 213-216; no one either good or bad, 270;

no one emotion the root of altruism, 301-302;

nonrational not unreasonable, 148-151; objections to

lists evaluated, 167-170; Plutchik's biological model

appraised, 137-142, 159-168; relation to appraisal,

147, 148, 152-156, 157, 158; relation to

consciousness, 180-182; relation to McDougall's view

178-181; relation to survival, 157-160; requirement

of irreducibility, 143-147, 161; summary of general

nature, 206-218, as unlearned motives, 133; verbal

problems, 132-134, 136, 137

Error, locus of, 79, 80

Fear-escape, definition defended, 255-257; related to

anxiety and guilt, 257-261